BRIDGES

by

Dixon Stalward

CABOOSE PRESS
Rocklin, CA 95677 USA

TO THE READER

The stories in this book are *entirely* fictional and must be approached in that way only. They are flights of fantasy and in no way are intended to serve as patterns for the very serious business of daily living. In acknowledging the harsh and unforgiving realities of the era of AIDS, you must protect *your* health, the health of our community, and that of humanity at large by engaging only in sexual practices deemed safe. Such safe practices must begin with, but are not limited to, adherence to an ironclad rule that there never, ever be any anal penetrations without condoms. *Absolutely!*

BRIDGES
by
Dixon Stalward

Table of Contents

BRIDGES

by

Dixon Stalward

This book is dedicated to our gay life.
Live it boldly and without apology.
There are no second chances.
Not even for today.

ONE

ORKNEY AND ME

I was out on the porch finishing up with my shaving.

It was about seven in the morning, and the canyon below was still deep in shadow but up higher the cliff was in full sun.

Orkney was down in the smokehouse cutting off a slab of our best bacon, the really prime stuff. That bacon and a couple of flats of brown eggs from our own hens was going to be our show of appreciation to Jim Fleetwood for the use of his pickup while our old International flat bed was temporarily out of commission after being stuck down there in the goddamned river.

And I mean *in* the river.

Maybe out of habit or maybe because something happened to catch my eye, I don't know, but anyway, when I looked up to where the trail comes to the cliff I saw the hikers. It's a clear view and if by chance you're watching, nobody can get across without being seen. Well, it didn't take a whole lot of looking on my part to tell that these hikers were the same three fellas, one black and two white, who'd come in once before.

And not too long ago either.

They were getting ready to start across the cliff.

Now, crossing that cliff is a fairly dangerous proposition. The trail, up to that point, is pretty good, but from there on it has no other way to go but across the cliff, and for about fifty yards or so it just hangs onto that sheer stone face with not much more than a few feet of ledge here and there to use the best way you can. Below, it's a straight drop of fifty feet or more to thick brush and a tumble of broken rock.

No sir, it's no place for morning strollers.

"Hey, Orkney," I yelled.

"Aye, Clement," Orkney yelled back. "What is it, luv?"

"It's them fellas coming in again. They're up there crossing the cliff right now."

"The three of them?"

"Yeah. The two white ones and the black one."

Orkney came up the steps carrying the bacon, a nice substantial piece smoked to a deep rich mahogany and thick with yellow fat. God, they never have anything like that at Safeway. Orkney hefted the meat like it was a prize he felt privileged in giving away.

"By the wee pigs of Aberdeen," he said in a wide grin, "good friend Jim will love this."

Jim Fleetwood, you see, is widely known as a big, big eater.

Orkney, being quite mindful of his own eating habits, has a slender physique—Jesus, elegantly so—on his tall frame, and he's also very, very handsome in his ruddy Scottish way. It always gives me a certain kind of precarious pleasure whenever he touches me, even in casual ways, and he did that then. Coming over to take a gander over at the cliff, he rested his arm across my shoulders.

Almost off the tight place now, the hikers were about to go down behind the sumac, greenish-gray and shadowy, and a stand so dense you can't see much of anything that's behind it.

But Orkney got himself a good enough look all right.

"Aye, 'tis sure enough," he said smiling in an inward sort of way he has when he's pleasantly surprised. "I really didn't think they'd come back."

I felt some of that pleasure too, but I also felt more than a little bit of apprehension.

I suppose it's best to say right off that Orkney's quite a bit younger than me. And in addition to that, the fella is much better educated and more cultured in the refinements to be found in the world, in the *larger* world. But that don't necessarily mean he's any smarter about *men* and *their* ways than me. No. It's always been my observation that, and for whatever reason, when you really come down to it there's not much in the way of mystery about men. Not really. But by God, there's sure as hell lots of room for suspicion. Maybe that's a murky thought, but it's something I just can't help feeling.

Anyway, a few months back, and for reasons I don't care to scrutinize, I started trying to talk and write like Orkney, to ape him I suppose you could say. Well, pretty soon he just up and told me it wouldn't work. He told me, and in some really nice words too, that I was the way I was. *And* that by *being* so, I was what *he* wanted. And *then* he went on to say that in his way of thinking I should be satisfied too if having him satisfied was in any way a help to me toward my own satisfaction.

Well, it was a mouthful all right, and when said out like that it did indeed help toward my own satisfaction. Of course I didn't just up and say that right out, but I was pretty sure Orkney knew though. He has a keen perception in personal matters, and he knows how to let his perceptions be known too.

"I wonder," Orkney said, and almost as if to himself, "if they'll be camping at the same place."

"I bet they will. I sure would."

"Oh, I know you would."

"My meaning here," I said, "is that *that* would be the place where they'd be most likely to see you."

Orkney's good-looking ears took on a rosy blush and he sort of ducked his head.

"Oh hell, Orkney," I said, "I'm not stupid. They didn't come back up here hoping to run into me."

"Now how do you know that?"

"Oh, I know all right."

And I really did know too. In a way.

Orkney, looking off to the side, nodded his head just a little.

You see, I've been up here in these mountains for more than twenty years, and, socially speaking, I'm kind of backward. Well, the truth is I was kind of backward even *before* I come up here. A part of me, the part of me still roaming around in the eighteenth century, would like to say that the time thus spent has been a period of primitive and pure introspection and

13

all that Walden Pond sort of stuff. But it hasn't. In quite a few ways—oh, in *more* than a few—it's been what you could call fulfilling, but mainly it's been hard. But then on account of that it's also been kind of... well, detached, and that detachment has given me valuable counsel in the transient nature of life. But even beyond all *that* it's been constant. I say constant in that I've never tried to or even wanted to foresee an end to it. But also in other areas that I'd always considered rather narrow, a life of this sort has always been vaguely wanting. And then, as time increased its pace, it became even downright lonely. Oh yes, it'd been *that* true enough. Yes. But even loneliness, I reasoned, like everything else was a condition that could be overcome by time and serene thoughts and so forth. Well, okay. I gave it a good shot, got through the tough part, and was doing all right until all of a sudden through circumstances I won't relate right now except to say that they were fortuitous, Orkney came into my life. Yep, the fella came into my life almost as if delivered by providence as a reward for all that deprivation. In speaking of providence I hasten to clarify that that's a use in a purely figurative sense of course. I've never had much truck with God, using the capital G for the sake of convenience. No, I've never messed with *that* God or with the makings of any *other* kind of deity either. Or, for that matter, I've never been sympathetic with any of those who might see fit to take up the gear and trappings of any sort of enterprise erected along religious lines.

But enough of that.

I really don't care much for blather. Not even my own.

In matters more pertinent let me say that in appearance I'm not what you'd call grizzled and that my baths aren't reckoned in terms of the seasons, but I'm still not the ruddily handsome, athletic, witty, congenial Scotsman that Orkney is. I am the older fellow, tall and thin, not dour but not inclined to smile at babies either, that some people expect to nod and then wait patiently at the end of the line. Which I do—when I really have to. But for the most part I don't because I see to it that I don't. So, keeping all that in mind you can see it wasn't me these three good-looking—and, Jesus, they were good-looking—hikers were coming around the mountain in hopes of seeing again.

No way.

In a vague sort of way I wished it otherwise, but probably not.

Orkney squeezed the back of my neck, gave my shoulder a solid punch, and stepped back to the table where he started wrapping the bacon in a brown paper sack.

He seemed to be busier at it than he needed to be.

"Well, Clement," he said, "I'd wager a wagon of wool that those fellows are just out seeing more of the country and getting in some exercise."

"Yeah, that might be so," I agreed.

Hell, we both knew damned well that it was a pretty rugged three mile trek up the ridge to that cliff, that there was plenty of other 'country' to be seen elsewhere, and that *these* fellas weren't in pressing need of any *sort* of 'exercise'.

But wait a minute.

But wait just a minute.

Let's go back a ways so's you can get a fuller picture. I don't want to loose you in confusion.

Earlier in the week Orkney and I had been on the river doing some fishing. We'd caught a jim-dandy string of trout—fine babies just the right size for a morning pan-fry—and were working our way downstream to where the river makes a tight bend into a narrow canyon. About half way in there's a really beautiful pool. It's our favorite place for swimming. The water's deep and there are ledges you can dive from, and from about as high as you could possibly want to go. I don't dive at all, but Orkney's got all kinds of guts in that area. I just hope I don't one day see them splattered on the rocks.

Anyhow, we'd entered the canyon but were still a ways away from the pool when I was pretty sure I heard voices—men's hollering voices—but it was hard to be certain on account of the noise made by the rapids.

I stopped.

"Orkney," I said, "I think there's people up there."

"Maybe. I expect we'll find out soon enough, won't we?"

I was pretty sure Orkney'd heard them too. He actually seemed eager, but that wasn't anything new. You see, Orkney, unlike me, enjoys encounters with strangers. Maybe it has something to do with his father being a preacher—parson he calls it—back in Scotland.

I don't know.

15

Anyhow, in a little further clarification, let me say this: some distance down the far slope there's this outfit called The Golden Creation Bible Institute, or some such thing, and once in a while people come up from there, but not too often on account of it being such a long hike. If you ask me those experiencing the calling to be preachers aren't usually much inclined toward *that* sort of exertion. Though, of course, I may be wrong. But like I say, once in a while two or three—or even a small group—do make the hike, and when he can Orkney likes to meet up with them and talk. I have a hunch he enjoys engaging them in theological discussion and in doing so show off his considerable savvy before he starts delivering some of these super-duper loopers he has along the lines of religious thought. Man alive, he can say some of the most harebrained things in the most logical and educated terms and make people believe he's serious. The fellow has what you'd have to call a brilliant intellect, and sometimes he uses it in the damnedest ways, hardly ever seriously, as if he considers being brilliant a part of a game, a game that's always changing.

It's really wonderful.

Anyhow, I thought maybe we were about to run into just such a bunch of bible nuts, and I just didn't want to.

Well, when we did get around the last tumble of boulders and looked down into the vicinity of the pool, why yes indeedy, there were people there. Oh yes.

Men.

Three of them, one black and two white.

And they were in the water.

In the wilderness it isn't wise to come up on people all of a sudden. Especially if, and preachers notwithstanding, they're men.

And so...

"Hello," I hollered out.

"Hello," someone hollered back.

I looked at Orkney.

"It's okay, Clement," he said. "Come on, let's go down."

So we made our way down to this long narrow catch of sand that has over the years been built up against a high rock face. It's always been a special place for me, and now it had the look of having been taken possession of, what with a tent, backpacks, clothes, and all the other clutter that comes along with hikers. Even though it was unreasonable and I knew it, I was a little pissed off because I felt that my personal territory had been staked out on.

Orkney didn't seem to be bothered at all. Right away he started getting undressed, apparently still planning on that swim.

I hunkered down to wait and see how things might go. Whenever experiencing vague doubt, I've found simple observation is sometimes the best bet.

Pretty soon one of the fellas—the African-American one—swam over near to where Orkney was and hauled himself out of the water onto a big rock.

He was naked.

"Hi there," he said.

I watched, suspicion turning a hard knot in my belly.

"Hi," Orkney replied.

He was a very handsome fella, this unwelcome visitor. His warm brown color was shockingly perfect on a body of uncommon excellence. He sat there with his legs hanging in the water and his hands on his knees while he watched Orkney undress.

"God, this is a fabulous place," he said waving his arm around like he was accustomed to making such pronouncements.

"Aye, friend," Orkney replied, "'tis a wonderful place all right."

"I sure hope we aren't intruding on you guys," the fella said flashing a dazzler of a smile. And I'll be damned if he didn't bat his big brown eyes when he added, "Are we?"

Orkney shook his head. "There's room enough for everybody."

And then looking at me he said, "There's more than enough room, isn't that right, Clement?"

Well, I nodded and said I guessed that was right.

The others had come closer and, treading water, were watching in a way that I could tell was cautious and not belligerent. Orkney waved and they waved back and said howdy.

"How are you fellows doing?" Orkney called.

They smiled and replied that they were doing fine.

Bending to push off his underwear, Orkney looked at me. "Are you coming in, Clement?"

17

"Naw. I'll watch out for bears," I said.

That got a round of appreciative laughter, boyishly loud.

I felt sort of paternal, dammit.

Then Orkney rose up, his superb body white and perfect there in that serenely beautiful place, and made a long shallow dive into the water. He come to the surface near the two fellas treading water and they exchanged watery greetings, short and slick, sort of like what you'd expect of seals, or of what *I'd* expect of seals in that I've been to the ocean exactly once. Anyhow, things seemed to be heading toward congeniality, and of course there really *was* enough room for everyone. Soon those young men were swimming and splashing, and doing some diving, sometimes together in two's and three's, and sometimes alone. It was a pretty sight in that way that makes you think everything is all right in the world even when you know it isn't. I mean in the short term. In the long term, in the cosmic sense, everything *is* all right because nothing wrong can last long enough to be wrong. Not that any of that makes a whit of difference in our everyday doings and efforts. Well anyhow, philosophy aside, my edginess, brought on by the presence of these strangers, started to subside a bit at a time, and I laid back and relaxed some. I got to thinking that maybe I'd go into the water after all, but then decided against it.

After a while the fellas hauled out on a large flat rock that slanted up from the water and sat there talking quietly among themselves. God, in natural poses and seemingly with all thought of style flung in the face of fashion, they were beautiful, what with the mantel of manliness laid across them like some deity with a deep yen for men folk had taken it upon himself to do some kind of special duty right then and there.

I gazed on them in a quiet sort of abstraction.

And then, by God in Christ's asshole, whatever purity or serenity there might have been in my thoughts was pushed aside when that ancient instinct of lechery began its crawl through my body, crawling with that warm heaviness of which there isn't but one kind. One kind. Indulging in the swiftest of speculations, I imagined what it would be like if those boys were to lay hands on each other and in doing so allow that same lechery, always on the crawl in all men, to bring up the passions that so often give life its most overwhelming and mysterious distress, a distress of sickeningly intense uncertainty. My cock, and it isn't no small thing, pushed down in

18

my underwear, pushed out in my pants. My asshole screwed shut, my balls went into a watery twist, and in no time at all my whole body was bound up in a tight coil ready to commence once again in the grapplings of the sexual adventure. Of course the possibility of things developing into anything at all in the way of grapplings was way, way more than remote.

But that didn't diminish the feeling one bit.

Oh hell no, not one damned bit.

Then the four of those handsome young men—everything that I, even on hands and knees, could have worshipped without shame—got to their feet and, standing in most benevolent postures as if they were on the steps of a church, started exchanging handshakes.

Orkney of course was doing most of the shaking.

And then he made another effortlessly perfect dive and swam his expert Australian crawl back toward me. Coming out of the water his chest was at a healthy heave. His eyes flashed and his smile was wide.

He flopped down at my feet.

"Their names are Manny, Moe, and Jack," he said.

"And they're just passing through. Right?"

"That's right. They're out here on summer vacation from somewhere in the east."

"Then they aren't preachers?"

Orkney grinned.

"Ho ho," he laughed. "There's not a parson in the lot."

Orkney was about to say something else when we heard big splashes, and pretty soon Manny, Moe, and Jack came out of the water and stood in a loose semi-circle a few feet away. Their legs were hard and muscular, their butts lean and tight. Water ran down their arms and dripped from their fingers. It ran down their chests to their bellies and into the hair below, and it dripped off the ends of their peckers drop by drop.

Drop by drop.

It was the pecker of one of them—the black one—that was uncut. Just the way that peter hung, pushed forward in a kind of possessive insolence, gave it a look that was particularly pagan and war-like. God, gleaming with a shockingly disturbing earthiness, it was, oh my, a handsome thing to look upon.

"So you fellas come out from the east?" I called as I stood up.

19

They watched me with a careful sort of attention.

"Yeah," one fella replied. He was the tallest of the three and had yellow hair and green eyes.

"Manny was through here last year by himself," he said. "He told us this was one helluva place."

"Which one of you is Manny?" I asked looking back and forth between the remaining two.

"That's me," the handsome black American said. "I'm Manny."

"I'm Moe," said the tall one.

"And I'm Jack," added the last.

Jack was slender through the torso and hips, but massive in the pins—particularly the thighs—like he was big competitor in the singular trial of field sports.

"And where would you fellas be going from here?" I said.

"Well," Manny said, "we'll probably go to Lake Magruder and spend a couple of days there exploring the salt caves. And from there we'll take the high trail through Majestic Gorge to Mile High Meadows and then over to Trident Falls."

"That's a trek of about a hundred miles," I said.

"Actually it's one hundred and twelve," Manny corrected.

I nodded.

"And it's fine hike too," Orkney said, looking at Manny and then at me. "Clement took me on it about a year ago. Not long after we met."

Manny sat down on the sand and leaned against a rock. His cock flopped out across the smooth brown skin of his thigh and there it lay glistening like a sleek talisman, a gift of impermanent wealth.

Moe went to a squat, his cock and balls hanging almost to the sand, and Jack fell into a sprawl, his legs folded together in a display of casual power.

Oh Jesus Christ, but there was a lot to look at! And despite my wariness I felt a surge of vague expectancy, the sort common in the meetings of men of differing inclinations. Not alien, just different.

Moe gazed at Orkney and me.

"No intrusion intended," he said, "but it seems to me that you two guys are doin' the time together."

"Doing time?" Orkney said.

20

Moe wrinkled his brow.

"Bein' partners, man," he clarified. "Bein' together."

"Aye, that we are, friend," Orkney replied. "That we are, and we're laying long term plans on it."

Orkney smiled at me.

Orkney's comment made me feel queerly special, as if I had no right to hear it.

Moe nodded his head slowly as if reconsidering the merits of an old proposition.

Then he said, "Oh, I suppose bein' together with somebody is a good enough deal all right. For the right sort of guys anyway."

"It's right for us," Orkney replied, smiling at me while sifting sand through his fingers.

Manny looked up at the ridge, angular, narrow, and rocky against the serene blue sky.

"Jesus," he said, "I know this would be the perfect place for me with the right guy. Just perfect. Once I thought I had the makings of something pretty damned good but—" and here he paused for the longest time—"but one afternoon he was waiting on the bus and got a bullet in the belly. And for nothing, man! All he had in the fucking brief case was tuna fish sandwiches and a couple of jelly donuts. Jesus Christ, his life for a brown bag lunch. Can you imagine? *God!*"

Manny's voice was harsh, almost shrill, on those last words.

A stiff silence grew among us as reminders of the pain to be found in the stark realities of life's caprices danced through our momentarily shared awareness.

"Oh Jesus," Manny said, his voice now in lower modulations, "I sure as hell didn't mean to bring that up. I really didn't. I'm sorry."

I wanted to say something nice to him, to demonstrate some sort of brotherhood of sympathy and hope and such, but then I suddenly realized that I was romancing with hogwash. What I *really* wanted was to *do* something *not* nice to him, something that would make his blackness *not* exotic to me, not a mantle of privilege, and in doing it render him the envelope—a very sexy envelope to be sure—of a more than likely amiable and probably playful—and funny—human being.

Jack lay back flat on the sand, an arm folded across his face, his legs

21

splayed. His cock, fat and looking as if it often managed big appetites, moved in a sort of torpid luxury. He put a hand to his groin. Fingering his balls, he then made a few passes over his cock before letting his hand come to rest low on his belly, fingers hooked into pubic hair.

From the corner of my eye I watched Orkney watch. In his steady blue eyes there was a kind of hunger I hadn't seen before. It was the hunger of a kind that's private—private in the most private of private reveries—and never spoken of.

Manny ran a hand up Orkney's leg to the calf. Stopping, he closed his fingers around the muscle.

"Oh man," he said, "you're so white. These other two dudes here are always so damned dark I forget they're white, and here you are the color of cool milk."

Moe glanced at me.

"Watch 'im," he said. "He'll be goin' for your dude's whang in another minute or so."

Looking directly at me Manny said, "No, I won't."

I felt a dizzy chill of threat bound up in a need for risk, and pushing and grunting along behind was that grinning old gent lechery, and now hung heavy with the silken ropes of possibility: Manny was fooling with Orkney but he was looking at me.

I felt wretched in a lovely way.

Very lovely.

Jack's hand went to his cock and stayed there, motionless but closed in a grip. His feet came up to his butt. His knees fell open, and there, not a scant inch up between his buttocks, lay the tightly bound brown hole that could with so little offer so damned much, and make good on that offer with so little effort.

Orkney's eyes were making flicking glances toward that hole.

Seeing so many inexplicit invitations developing—and not even sure of my own *civilized* reaction—I felt in my belly a churning of incredibly greedy desires. And at the same time a certain evil possessiveness rode me for I knew without a doubt that Orkney was, and most likely even more that me, caught in that same twisting churn, and *that* was something I *did not want* to be so.

Manny's hand was still resting on Orkney's leg.

"You don't come out in the sun much, huh?" Manny said.

Orkney looked down at his white body, it's whiteness always stunning to me.

"I burn." he said.

"Yeah, I bet you do," Manny replied.

Manny looked at me and smiled. "This is one sharp fella you have here, Clement."

I nodded.

Jack pulled his hand from his cock. It had gone to a full erection, and as it stood there tall and straight I could see this very sexy ruff of skin just below the head.

Jack was exhibiting himself with the serenity of a monk.

"Oh oh," Moe said, "Jack's got his rod run up."

"I'm just relaxing," Jack replied. "It don't mean a thing."

"Oh ho ho," Manny said. "Nope, not a thing."

"Now didn't I just say I was relaxing?" Jack repeated.

"Okay, pull your legs up and open your butt and we'll see how relaxed you are," Moe said.

Jack took his arm from his face. He looked up at Orkney.

"Jesus," he said, "I'm really not that easy."

"Oh God, Jack," Moe said, "modesty, especially that phony kind, don't become you."

And then Jack, smiling sweetly as if he hadn't heard Moe and still looking at Orkney, said, "But in some cases I can be easier than pie. Sweet cherry pie."

"Cherry pie!" Moe laughed. "My dear, you're *always* easier than any kind of pie."

Moe got to his knees holding his cock. It was well up to an impressive erection.

"Open up, baby," he said to Jack.

"No."

"Yes!"

"No," Jack repeated. "Things aren't right yet."

"Well, we'll get them right."

Jack shook his head slowly and said in a low voice, "When there's any fucking going to be done it's going to be done by *him*, dammit!"

I looked at Orkney, the obvious *him* here. His face was twisted with lascivious delight. His lips were pulled wide in a mirthless grin as hard as iron and as substantial as a fart.

Manny had risen to one knee and his hand was advancing up Orkney's thigh. Orkney's cock was responding in the usual way, and I felt a pang of regret. But that was quickly pushed forward into the lock of our personal intimacy as a sea of possibility rose up behind it. I too could possibly be caught up and loose myself in this little whirlpool of passion that was developing so rapidly.

Catching my eye, Orkney raised his brow and shrugged his shoulders as if to dismiss the guilt of millions while unable to mask his own crouched there as it was in the sharp relief of very keen desire.

Manny had Orkney's scrotum in his hand.

And then...

Oh golly.

And then three big dogs, two red hounds and a mastiff—their barks high and short—bound out of nowhere and made straight for Orkney.

"Jesus Christ!" Manny shouted, scrambling to his feet.

Jack and Moe quickly followed suit as the dogs closed in on Orkney.

Orkney got to his knees, his arms wide.

"Hey! Hey, you guys!" he yelled, trying to throw a full tackle on all three dogs at once. Playfully evading that display, the dogs feinted this way and that and then came in to stand—panting like the devil—to get the attention they wanted.

"Where the fuck did *they* come from?" Jack exclaimed, his face *and* his cock drained of all bravado.

"They belong to Ranger Jim Fleetwood," I said.

"And he'll be coming along in just a minute," Orkney said, himself a little breathless.

And of course Ranger Jim was indeed shortly on the scene.

Mounted high on his silver gelding named Saint, Chief Ranger Jim Fleetwood rode out of a cleft in the canyon wall and cantered, horse hooves in a clicketty clatter on the sliding pebbles, toward our largely naked little group. Crisply efficient looking—not to mention goddamned handsome—in his dun and black uniform, Jim reigned up about six feet away. Under a Smoky Bear hat his dark eyes darted from one naked body to another.

"Now, Clement," Jim said, "how come is it that you're the only man here that's still got his clothes on?"

I pushed my hands in my back pockets and shrugged my shoulders feeling awfully dumb.

"It does," Jim said, "seem sorta odd to me."

"Hi, Jim," Orkney called, himself now quite recovered in his self-control. "These fellows are Jack, Moe, and Manny."

"How do, fellas," Jim greeted putting his fingers to his hat. "But, fact is, I already know you. Not by your names of course. I seen you yesterday mornin' when you was workin' your way along the saddleback to the ridge trail. You make good time."

After exchanging quick glances, Manny, Moe, and Jack said howdy to Ranger Jim Fleetwood.

Jim smiled. His wide country face was a display of abundant goodwill, the goodwill of authority, and he had, hanging on the belt around his sturdy midsection, all the gear necessary to back up that authority. Among us locals, the man was, in a way, imperial. Being large—six feet six inches of solid muscle laid over with a substantial layer of insulation—was just the beginning of that imperial stance. But beyond that, he wasn't inclined to allow much of anything to contradict his observations and perceptions, and those were usually pretty well founded in fact. Our county, in terms of the Ranger Service, was Chief Ranger Jim Fleetwood's kingdom, and there wasn't much that went on in it that he didn't know about if he wanted to.

"Now, fellas," Jim said, "as much as I'd like to relax here and chat, we ain't got a whole lotta time for it right now."

He looked at me.

"Ole Dewey Patch called me on the radio, Clement. He says that even as we speak your flatbed is standin' in about four feet of water."

I looked at Orkney.

"Oh shit," he said, "it sounds like that brake has failed again."

"Reckon so from what I hear," Jim said.

"Hell, I should have blocked the damned wheels," I muttered.

We'd parked our truck at the usual place on the slope above River Forks, and apparently the brake had failed again. It did last week and the truck had rolled about eight feet before hitting a tree. Now it sounded like it was in the river.

25

"Well," Jim said, "I told ole Patch to call in a tow truck right quick, but you'd better skeedaddle up there and secure your vehicle in some way if you can. Them rocks is on sand and have a way of shiftin' under any sudden new weight. Give that river a little time and you might never get your vehicle out again, tow or no tow."

"That's the truth," I said. "I've got a sixty foot length of cable in the rigging box. That'll do the job."

"Sounds like it to me," Jim replied.

In just a couple of minutes Orkney was dressed and ready to go.

Manny, Moe, and Jack were standing around looking on in that awkward way of strangers who haven't yet had time to tune in on local ways and affairs.

"Is there something we can do to help?" Manny asked.

"Thanks for asking," I said, "but we can handle it okay."

Manny put out a hand.

"Well then," he said, "maybe we'll be seeing you guys again."

"It'd be something to look forward to," Orkney said.

We all made a round of handshakes with Jim Fleetwood looking on, his eyes sweeping across the naked bodies, across their butts, their bellies, their cocks.

"It's a shame to be bustin' up the party," he said.

Jack looked up at the big ranger.

"That's the truth," he said.

"Maybe we'll be coming through again," Manny said.

"Might could even count on it," Moe said.

He was looking at Orkney.

Perhaps caught in an awkward squeeze between desire and decorum, Jim Fleetwood fidgeted a little and then touched his hat and called his dogs and went back toward the cleft where he paused just a moment and then departed to his duties on the ridges.

I gathered our gear and set off on the up river hike.

In a few minutes I heard Orkney hurrying to catch up.

"We could have let them help," he said.

"We can do it ourselves."

"I know, but they could have helped anyway."

I have to admit now as I did to myself then, but in an oblique sort of way, that I was jealous and upset in several ways, the most distressing being faced with the ambiguous threat that Orkney might have shown in some way or another an interest in one of those fellas that could result in his being taken from me. In reality probably not, but still I was certain I'd seen the makings of that catastrophe, and I was, to put it simply, scared shitless at just the thought. I felt the need of safety that could be found only in retreat and in that retreat, silence. But even more subtle, but no less damaging, was the guilt I felt in wanting something—just something—for myself and by myself, with Orkney put off someplace safely and securely untouchable.

Selfish. Oh yes, selfish. And selfish in the most basic human way.

Well, when we got back to River Forks, the truck wasn't in such a bad way after all.

Oh, it wasn't good by any means, but it wasn't all that bad either.

The water it was in wasn't as deep as it could have been. Another two or three feet further and the cab would have been under for sure. But the real problem lay in the fact that the right wheels, front and back, were hanging into a channel and both axles were resting on a big rock. And to worsen the matter a little the current there was pretty stiff.

Oh boy, it was going take one hell of a big son of a bitch of a tow to budge that truck.

Orkney, not being so used to such difficulty, shook his head.

"God, Clement," he said. "Oh Jesus, I don't know how..." and then his voice trailed off.

"We'll manage all right," I said. "It's going to be tough, but we'll manage."

So as to keep things from getting any worse, we followed Jim's advice and secured the truck to a cottonwood tree using a double cable loop and a cinch chain.

"Good enough," I said.

Knowing it'd be at least an hour or so waiting on the tow, we sat down on some rocks amongst a stand of deer sage. The breeze was warm and moved through the short, stiff leaves making a sort of soft scratching sound.

"What'd you think of those fellows, Clement?" Orkney asked after a while.

"Oh, they were nice enough, I'd say."

There was another pause.

"How far do you think things might have gone if Jim hadn't shown up?" Orkney said.

"Oh, I imagine things would have gone just about as far as they could," I said, "and then some."

Orkney sort of sighed as if the victim of a soft betrayal.

"Christ," I said, "those fellas were so hot for you they'd have waded through cold shit just to get close enough for a grope."

"That's an unfortunate way of putting it."

And it certainly was.

"Sorry," I said.

Orkney looked away.

The pause was long, and then the silence that followed was thicker than any I could remember. I couldn't think of one damned thing to say to cut through it. Christ, I felt like I could have counted my heart beats one by one and, goddammit, forever.

After a while Orkney said, "Would you have done anything?"

"Well, I was waiting on you, Orkney."

"Did you want to?"

I shrugged, my dishonesty fitting uncomfortably well.

"It was obvious that is was you they were interested in," I said.

"I'm not so sure about that. I was waiting on you."

I leaned back into the sage. The smell was sharp and intense, bitter and enticing.

"Well," I said, "all that's over now."

"Yes, I suppose so."

Orkney went to his knees.

"I could help us—you and me—pass the time," he said. "Are you still loaded up?"

"Well, yeah. Are you?"

"Yes."

Orkney put his hands on my thighs and I opened my pants. My cock jumped out as if a willful charlatan awaiting an opportunity to work a little mischief.

Orkney took it in hand and looked up.

"I was thinking how I'd liked to have seen you put this baby up Jack's butt, " he said. "God, Clement, you could have made him squirm on it put up that hard ass of his."

"Do you think so?"

"I know so."

"Well, maybe... "

Then he bent and took my charlatan into his mouth, and it was a charlatan no more. Holding my balls like they were precious gifts, he went to the root in a single downward push. His head rose and fell in the regular pattern of skillful cock sucking. I helped in the doing of the job by raising up my hips to meet his movement. We worked at the ambiguous effort for several minutes, and soon enough I could feel the tingle in my dick, that little dance of fugitive promise, signaling that the payoff was close to coming up.

"I'm going to shoot pretty damned quick, Orkney," I whispered.

Pulling up from my cock, Orkney looked at me and in his pretty blue eyes I saw that urgent need.

"Then come just for me, Clement," he said in a flat voice. "Just for me. I want to suck down that heavy, slick load of jizz you could have pumped up Jack's ass."

And then going back to the hot, wet duty he sucked with an élan seated in the exquisite homosexual debauchery. His handsomeness, his wholesomeness, the sweep of maleness that made him special, the perfect equilibrium that defined his life, were all subordinated to the base endeavor, the ignoble ideal—thrust high on the pikes of opprobrium—to be found in the male sucking of male cock, and, in the here and now of it, my male cock. Feeling the silky execution being prepared for me in his mouth, relishing the fervor of his seeking of this enactment of trade, I was on the edge of elation, yet in the crease of despair, as the summons of the jizzy-gift came ever closer to success.

It was mine, and then it wasn't.

It was.

And then it wasn't.

I spread my legs.

I flexed my buttocks.

"Put a finger up my asshole, baby," I whispered.

29

Orkney's hand found its way through my crotch, between the fold of my buttocks, and to that curlicue of flesh, the threshold to our queer heaven. That finger, by no description savage, made its probes against the rubbery ring of hidden love.

And few... Oh lord!

And few were needed to send the bucket into the well.

"Shit!" I gasped.

The turning of the screws and the tightening of the nuts were finished. The ancient silliness, the ludicrous loveliness, had worked its bent miracle one more time, and this new dose of jizz, triggered by Orkney's finger in my asshole and launched from deep in my belly, shot into the diligent man's mouth with a hot velocity, direct, simple, and very, very evident. I thrust upward and felt the roll of gag and retch as the stuff was pumped into Orkney's mouth, into his throat, the head of my dick delivering the gobs as if they even as benevolent gifts were bound up with antipathy.

In a minute it—all of it—subsided as it always does, and I felt that hollow, grateful feeling of wistful betrayal.

Orkney looked up.

He was breathing heavy, and his eyes were bright. Those of a fox.

"Good fucking load," he said. "Outstanding. God, taking a load of your jizz always makes me so fucking hot!"

The last of his highlander's rectitude—always rather precarious—was slipping into the ditch.

And fast.

Standing, he opened his Levis and his erected cock, the head a hard magenta knob, sprung into my face. I put my mouth on it. Being in that mood of mellow, if counterfeit, contrition I set right into the suck as if I had until doomsday. The boner, oh so familiar in size and shape, filled my mouth to capacity. Using my well-practiced technique I eased it down into my throat.

Ah yes, by the grace of God granted in perversion, I felt the king of homosexual fellatio—there being, of course, a definite difference from the *other* kind—as I cradled, nursed, and adored that cock in my throat. But even with that I knew it wasn't the time to dawdle with refinements of technique.

"Get at those nuts too," Orkney croaked.

Still not in a great hurry, but soon enough to keep the effort moving in a smooth forward flow, I went on to the testicles. Taking the little simpletons into my mouth, first one at a time and then as a pair, I let them just sort of float on my tongue so's to enjoy them in their soft, simple, and effortless existence

I jacked Orkney's cock.

"Chew," he said.

He didn't really mean 'chew' as in 'masticate', and I knew it.

What it was that he liked was the feeling of being gently consumed, a consuming where the teeth, in tender precaution, moved in a chewing motion of an amiable sort while the tongue, like a solicitous viper, busied itself pushing here and there, a steward in the consumption.

And that's what I did.

Expertly.

"That's good nut sucking," Orkney said, his voice a rolling goose of highland encouragement. "Good sucking."

I nodded the best I could knowing that, by the tails of horny monkeys, I *was* doing a good job.

"Oh yes, good sucking."

He rolled his hips.

"Oh yes, good nut sucking."

I pushed his Levis to his knees and put my hands on the lovely round buttocks. Running my hands over those splendid muscles, I felt the power of fuck resting there in repose. Then he pulled up, those hot eggs slipping from my mouth, and gave my face a few slaps with the head of his dick. I could feel the thin, hot threads of the exquisite ooze spatter across my nose and lips, then slide down and drip to my chin. I sent my tongue out, ambitious and able, to get as much of the silvery slop as I could. The dickhead, the magenta now a glare of red and orange, bulged with authority, the slit a squinty, suspicious bitch. With my tongue broad and soft I licked the dick in slow, deliberate strokes until Orkney grunted in satisfaction, and then I went stiff and pointed against the hole, useful in the making of friendly little threats against it, the threats of abuse nested in the careful weave of trust. My lips soon followed with a tight, moist embrace, my tongue once again doing the mindlessly repetitive dance of a snake.

"And now, piss hole kisser," Orkney muttered, "take a suck at some asshole. Get in my butt and suck asshole."

He turned and bent forward, and I opened the cheeks to the round, brown splendor of his asshole. It beckoned to me with a casual twist, a demure inward suck. With my trusty tongue at the ready I put my mouth against it and entered into the soft degradation, the heady thrill, of the anal kiss. He smelled of sweaty underwear, fresh mountain water flushed with trout shit, thick green moss, and waterlogged wood heavy and doomed. The tight, smooth tissue was of the texture of ancient silk, and in that curious kiss—curiouser for my love of it—there lay forsaken hope recovered.

For he, Orkney and his asshole, my temple of lust, tasted of love.

"That's good. Fucking Jesus hung on the cross, that's good."

While I sucked asshole, moving on from pothole to post, Orkney squirmed his butt back against my face while running a jack off on his cock in an effort to build this matter into the velvety monster he had in mind.

"For all the king's glory, the fine mountain man is sucking me fucking bung."

The hole did a curtsy of a twist, perhaps a cousin to a fart.

"He's sucking bung for the squirt of sweet, sweet highland cream."

The hole pushed out, my tongue pushed in.

"The parson's son's got a bung full of mountain man tongue."

The hole got looser and then went tight again The buttocks stiffened on my face.

"The parson's pride is going to shoot!"

I twisted my tongue in his anus, going for golden apples.

"The parson's pride's got it!"

Pulling away from me, Orkney turned and, his legs bent, his one hand working the jack off on the mighty cock and the other cupping the balls, put the head to my face and delivered the promised jizz. Coming in majestic spurts, the first hit the side of my nose, the second my upper lip, the third made the shot straight into my mouth, the fourth oozed out of the cockhead with imperial perfection. My tongue reaching out in welcome, my lips then embraced the crimson orb to usher in the quiet conclusion to another of our healthily perverted celebrations.

Well then, it took us two days and three tries with two different rigs to get that truck out of the river, but by God we did it. Jim Fleetwood drove by ever so often to see how things were going. He was there when the Load

Lugger 555 Tri-Rig—one big son of a bitch—finally got the job done. It was when we were getting the flat bed ready for the haul up the hill to our place that Jim made the generous offer of the use of his pickup for as long as we needed it.

"God, we'd certainly appreciate it, Jim," Orkney said.

"All somebody's gotta do," the big man said, "is give me a lift up to the station and then the truck is yours."

Orkney assigned that responsibility to me.

So Jim and I set off through Pinnacle Rocks and up the long grade to the ranger station.

"Now tell me, Clement," Jim said after we'd gone a distance, "them fellas that you was with in the canyon the other day, be they friends of you and Orkney's?"

"No. We'd just met them."

"God, from the look of things I'd'a sworn you all was workin' up to a party situation."

I felt a hot rush of blush when I said, "I guess that's the way it looked, Jim, but nothing happened."

Jim ran his hand up the inside of his massive thigh and took a good grip on his bulging crotch.

The man's action was direct, but not greasy with sneaky insinuation. He was much too self-possessed—too big—for that. He was getting ready to make a point.

"I ain't never made no approach to you and Orkney because I figgered you two was private fellas. Then I seen you down there at the river—five of you for Christ's sake!—and I figgered that maybe an orgy situation was developin', that it was somethin' you and Orkney did after all. And such a good-lookin' bunch of rascals you were too!"

"Oh yes," I agreed, "they were fine looking fellas, all right."

Jim clapped his hands and laughed.

"Man oh man, let me tell you, Clement, it's in an orgy situation that I find *my* meat! Jesus Christ, I coulda ate every lovely part and hole of the whole lovely bunch of you!"

God, just as in everything else the man was enthusiastic and nothing if not voracious.

Jim looked at me and grinned.

33

"Well, Jim," I said, "Orkney and me haven't done that before, but that don't mean we won't."

Jim grunted in a way of satisfaction.

"That's good enough for me," he said. "I ain't gonna press for nothin' specific, but just so's you know, I got the place when—and if—the time is right."

"Well, Jim," I said, "I'll bring the subject up with Orkney when the occasion seems right."

Jim grunted again, and nodded his head. "I can't beat that."

And then in a minute he said, "Just be sure and tell Orkney that I intend no intrusion on your lives. Or anybody else's. I'm just a big old honker who likes to get in on an orgy situation now and then. Keep on my toes, if you get my meanin'."

"Right."

I dropped Jim at the ranger station promising to return his pickup just as soon as our flat bed was up and running.

And that wasn't very long either.

In two days we changed all the wiring and filters, repacked the parking brake, put in wheel kits, bled the lines, did a major tune-up and a carburetor overhaul, drained the radiator and ran a core check, and, finally, put in a rebuilt starter, which was about due anyway.

The old tank was as good as new. Well, almost.

Off the blocks and off the jack, the truck seemed to offer as new partnership as it sat there in the slanting rays of the late afternoon sun. I like being in the garage at sundown. The shadows are dark and definite, the place has an ancient smell like it was never new, and you know that soon enough you'll be out of there. I was sorting through the old parts, and had me two neat piles: one was definitely junk and the other was more or less borderline. Orkney was taking care of the last details on the truck, you know, wiping mirrors, cleaning small things, doing the thoughtful stuff that makes a good job perfect. He was stripped down to his white boxer underwear, and the way he moved to accomplish his tasks—fluid and easy like a dancer—made me think that maybe he really wasn't aware of his own beauty.

"You know, Clement," he said, "maybe we'd ought to paint this truck. Give it a lift."

"And what color would you paint it, Orkney?"

"I'd choose red. A bright, bright red."

"Red! Why, they'd see us coming from all over the county."

"They see us coming already, Clement."

I gave several things a few fast thoughts, and then pitched all the used parts into a fifty gallon drum. There's not much point in hanging onto old broken things that don't work.

"You're right of course, Orkney," I said. "Sure, let's paint the truck. Sometimes it's good to make a change."

"Red?"

"You bet red, and the brightest red they make."

I smiled and then took a deep breath.

"There's something I was thinking about too," I said.

"What's that?"

"It isn't too easy to say."

"Then just say it, Clement."

"Okay. Do you like knowing you make men hot?" I said. "I'm talking about other men besides me."

"What other men besides you?"

"Well, any of them."

Orkney cocked his head.

"Can you be more specific?" he said.

"Well, like those fellows down at the river. Manny, Moe, and Jack, to be specific. And maybe Jim Fleetwood."

Orkney sat down on a camp stool and leaned forward. The fly of his boxers lay open enough to afford me a peek at the head of his dick. God, just that small glimpse of the lovely organ in its soft repose and knowing that I had access to the whole thing—and hard!—as well as anticipating what I was about to propose started my juices flowing.

"Aye, Clement," Orkney said, "I enjoy being attractive to men. To men in general, and to certain ones specifically. Though I must say I don't much set the beat of my heart on it. It's a flimsy game. Sure, meeting Manny, Moe, and Jack was exciting. And Jim Fleetwood... well, Jim's quite a man all right. He could sure as hell hold his own against any highland chieftain I ever met. Aye, Jim Fleetwood's quite a man."

Orkney cocked his head and grinned.

"And you say he's hot?"

I nodded. "Oh yes, he's hot all right. To trot."

"With whom?"

"Well, the likes of Manny, Moe, and Jack to begin with. And you. And me too apparently."

"Ho ho! That's quite a list. It sounds like the man's a gang-banger. When did you find all this out?"

I shrugged.

"Oh just the other day," I said. "When he lent us his pickup."

Orkney nodded.

"And he wants to bang with us?" he said.

Though the phrase was kind of new to me I knew what Orkney meant. I nodded.

"But," I said, "he's very emphatic about not making any sort of intrusion. It seems he likes to get in on what he calls an orgy situation. That's it and nothing more."

"Really?"

"Yeah."

I paused and then said, "Would you go for it? To be specific, I mean go for a meeting with Jim Fleetwood and you and me?"

Orkney looked down, and then up, his blue eyes serious.

"Yes," he said. "And would you be so inclined?"

"Yeah, I think so."

Orkney sighed.

He looked across the garage and squinted his eyes as if trying to count the nail heads in the wall.

"Scotland was a lonely place for me as a youngster," he said. "Everything was always done so seriously. Even lust. *When* it was done. And there I was, this horny parson's boy with I suppose more curiosity, *and* inclination, than was good for him, but without even a blind fly's idea of how to go about doing anything about it. When something *did* happen it was more than likely to be swamped in the same old wallow of highland ignorance that surrounded everything about human touching that wasn't expected to draw blood. And then the guilt! We mustn't forget the goddamned guilt; there were variations on the variations. And so, to shorten a short story, when I'd finally liberated myself from the peat bogs of gentle but persistent hypocrisy I concluded that it was not wise, lustfully speaking of course, to pass up any healthy opportunity. And that, these many wonderful years later, would include Jim Fleetwood should the occasion arise."

"And would that include Manny, Moe, and Jack? Speaking on speculation of course."

"Aye, my friend."

I sat in silence thinking that over.

I had little difficulty in getting a handle on a 'deal' with Jim Fleetwood. I knew him. He was my age, and I pretty much knew what he was about. Well, God, he'd come right out and laid his cards on the table when he'd considered the situation right. But the other three were a different matter entirely. They were young, handsome, unknown, and in being all that they represented not a little danger.

As if reading my thoughts, Orkney began to talk, "I guess now is the time to draw a distinction, Clement, between what amounts to little more than recreation and that which is important in the matter of serious commitment building. Anything that's likely to happen between us and Jim Fleetwood—and those other three fellows or anybody else like them—falls into the category of recreation. What transpires between the two of us falls into the other, and since it's a lot more complicated than recreation it is, therefore, more meaningful. That of course is by no means the whole of it. But, in ways that are themselves kind of complicated, the two impulses, that of recreation and that of commitment, are somehow connected."

Listening to Orkney, I gazed on the truck, visualizing it red. But beyond being red or whatever color, it was *our* truck. Sometimes Orkney drove it, and sometimes I did, but it was always our truck. And now it was to be red, and very probably a bright red.

So what?

"I think I get your drift, Orkney," I said.

"We're together, Clement, and in some ways we're also apart."

I nodded.

"Well, let's talk more about it later," Orkney said. "Right now though, how about some supper? I put some pork chops in the oven."

"Okay. Tomorrow we can take Jim's pickup back to him and then maybe go on to town and see about getting this truck painted red."

"Good enough."

"Let's do something jazzy with the interior too."

"Like what, Clement?"

"Like getting all black leather upholstery—the works—and maybe a spacey sound system too."

"Whoa there, Clement," Orkney said. "Let's just think about red paint for now, okay?"

And we went into supper.

It was those pork chops baked with apples.

So, that's how all that happened. I hope I didn't loose you.

It was the next morning when we were fixing to return Jim's pickup to him, and make a gift of the bacon and eggs, that I spied Manny, Moe, and Jack coming across the cliff, and had called down to Orkney in the smokehouse.

Well, after that talk we'd had in the garage and after I'd had an opportunity to think about it over night, I suddenly had a lot of ground to cover. I mean talking and thinking were one thing. Acting was quite another. And here I was faced with that very thing.

While Orkney was getting our gifts packed in a shopping bag, I sat down on the willow settee to pull on my boots.

I tried to sound casual when I said, "Them fellas will be down at the river in about a half hour or so. Maybe we could stop by there. If we should see them, we could say hello. And maybe we could even take time for a swim."

Orkney came to stand beside me. He put his hand on the back of my neck and squeezed.

"That's sounds like a good idea," he said, "if it's something you feel comfortable with."

"I do."

"They're good-looking guys," he said, "and they're probably fine men, too, but they don't hold a candle to you, Clement."

I stood up.

"Well," I said, "be assured that Jim Fleetwood's sure got a hankering after them."

"The whole bunch?"

"Yep, the whole hot bunch."

38

Orkney laughed.

God, he was handsome.

"Well, Jim's a tough old bear," he said, "and so you've got to figure him for a big appetite."

"I suspect it's as big and wide as these mountains."

I put my hand on Orkney's shoulder. "Look, I don't know a whole lot about this game of sharing bodies and such, but if things work out like that I'll go along."

"It's not important, Clement."

"Probably not in the long haul, but in the short one it could be. I mean, it seems the immediate satisfactions to be found in a passing moment can be of help in sustaining the more important things."

"Do you really believe that, Clement?"

"I do. I've thought about it, and I do."

Actually I hadn't thought about it a whole lot in such specific words, but when I said it I realized that I had, and I knew that I believed it.

"Let's go take a swim," Orkney said.

So we, Orkney and me, him going ahead in the pickup and me following in the flat bed, came down off our mountain, went through Bluebell Meadows, and along the river to Rock Arch Bridge.

Well, and in the damnedest of all possible coincidences as only chance could arrange, on the far end of the bridge there were three hikers, and they, I realized as we drew closer, were, of all people, Jack, Moe, and Manny.

Of course we, Orkney and me, stopped the trucks and got right out.

"Hello," Orkney called.

He got three enthusiastic responses.

Manny made an easy vault up to the bridge.

"Hi there, Clement," he said. "Nice to see you again."

Surveying the trucks he said, "I'll bet it was one of these that was in the water the other day."

"Yeah," I said. "It was that old flat bed there. The pickup belongs to Jim Fleetwood."

"The ranger man, huh?" Jack said.

"That's right."

"Jesus Christ, what a man! What an *enormous* man." Jack replied.

39

"God, he could... "

"I bet he could," Moe interrupted, "and I *know* you'd let 'im."

"Why hell yes, Moe, and I know you'd just love to look on too."

I looked at Orkney. He shrugged his shoulders and smiled.

"We're taking Jim's truck back to him now," I said. "Why don't you fellas come along for the ride. Come up and visit the ranger station."

"I'd call that a deal to go for," Jack said.

"You bet," Moe agreed.

So Jack and Moe climbed into the pick up with Orkney. Manny got in with me, and we all set out for a visit to the ranger station and, probably, Jim Fleetwood.

Manny's was wearing cut-off Levis, and his legs were long and shapely. Sitting there with worldly poise in the jumble and clutter of my old workaday truck I was caught again by the desire to make gentle—several gentle—assaults on his body.

"You're a sexy man, Clement," he said. "I hope Orkney takes care of you properly."

Christ, I almost lost control of the truck.

"He does," I stammered.

"Good."

Moving down in the seat Manny put his feet up on the dashboard. His knees were spread wide.

"But if there's ever a time when he doesn't," he said, "I can."

"With your legs up like that?"

"You bet. Up like this, or any other way you might want."

It took only a short glance at his slender legs and lovely butt to convince me to keep my eyes on the road.

Manny went on, "But to be even blunter, Clement, could something like that be arranged sometime?"

"Yes, I think so."

It wasn't all that big a leap into the world of sexual sophistication but it was still enough to make me dizzy. I felt an imminent threat—curiously comfortable—of change.

In the truck ahead three handsome heads bobbed about in animated conversation.

When we drove into the station yard Jim was sitting on the porch in his underwear. He was tying fishing flies. Putting aside his work, he stood, his mighty body a mountain of capability, and put a foot up on a porch rail. The underwear, white briefs pleasingly tight, bulged in all the right places with the masculine presences.

The man's smile could have lighted all of God's heaven.

"Well, I'll be goddamned!" he shouted as we piled out of the trucks, "what a helluva nice surprise."

"Now it wouldn't be the governor you're expecting, would it, Jim Fleetwood?" Orkney asked, taking in the man's stout figure.

"No it ain't," Jim replied, "but if it was this would still be my attire if I felt like it."

"Then we aren't intruding, sir?" Jack said fixing his gaze on Jim in a way that was even more than intent.

"Hell no, young fella." Jim's eyes rested on the fellows shoulders and then went to his hips. "Your name's Jack, ain't it."

"Yes sir."

"Now listen here, Jack," the ranger said, "there ain't no need for the formality of you calling me 'sir'. In my official capacity or otherwise, just plain Jim will do nicely."

Orkney took the few steps up to the porch.

"I'm going into the kitchen, Jim," he said. "There's a little something for you here in the bag."

Jim's eyes lighted up. "Why thank you, Orkney. I do thank you."

Orkney went inside.

There were a few seconds of hesitant smiles, of darting glances.

"Well hell," Jim boomed, "let's *everybody* go inside where we can all sit down and chat some."

Jim led the way inside, his huge legs at a stomp.

The station office was one large and comfortable room. Eschewing any tendency toward self-indulgence or ostentation, the furnishings—sized for giants—were simple in design and direct in function, and mostly things crafted by mountain people. All except for a towering Chinese chest arrogant in its brass and red lacquered grandeur and an enormous iron bed, cobalt blue in color. They were situated in a far corner beneath the low hang of a loft. The bed, with its expanse covered with a thick satin comforter and hills of colorful pillows, was a sprawl of invitation.

41

"God, what a bed," Jack said, approaching it with a confident stride, a certain swagger in the hips.

Jim followed by a close step.

"I'm told that that there bed," he said, "was once the pride and joy of a turn of the century whorehouse in San Francisco. They say it belonged to the manager of the male division."

"Really?" Jack said, apparently at the moment very much willing to believe almost anything.

"Oh hell, Jack," Jim said, his face an exaggerated frown, "I don't know." He paused. "But what I really *do* know for a fact, young fella, is that this bed belongs to *me* now."

Jim put a possessive hand on the head frame.

"Yep, it's mine all right," he said, "and most of what gets in it is too."

"Neat-o," Jack said falling back into the voluminous embrace of whispering satin.

Jim sat down on the edge of the bed and started unlacing Jack's hiking boots.

"I do like your boots, kiddo," he said, "but not in my bed."

Jack's boots quickly thumped to the floor

"I've always liked," Jack said scooting to the center of the bed, "having lots of room to move around in." He pushed a huge pink pillow behind his back and settled against it.

"And I like things big." he said. "Big."

Jim lay down on the bed and drew one leg up, the thigh as thick as a road post.

"Most things come pretty big around here," he said.

"That's what I figured," Jack replied.

Manny took a step or two toward me.

"I'll bet *that's* big too," he said looking at my crotch.

I could feel the primitive stirring in my pants. But that feeling of precaution—no, of apprehension—rode on my shoulders still. I looked at Orkney. He was standing in the kitchen doorway looking at Moe who had flopped down on a fort-like couch upholstered with cowhide.

"Well, shit," Moe said looking up at Orkney with a sophomoric leer, "I ain't shy. I'll suck the first dick that gets shoved in my mouth. The first one, man. And I'm good at it too."

Moe ran his hands back and forth across the smooth cowhide at his sides, the movement soothing, encouraging.

"God, I like this," he said. "Feels good."

Stepping down from the kitchen door, Orkney opened his pants and pushed his hand through the white gap in his boxer shorts.

Moe watched for a second and then looked up.

"I bet it glows like a Christmas tree," he said.

"Yes, I suppose it does," Orkney replied.

"I'm a guy who always did like Christmas."

Orkney produced his cock. The head glowing as promised, it's mouth, sulky and red, was wet with that magic spit of desire.

Moe took a firm grip on the shaft with one hand and put the other through the boxer fly.

"Would it," he said, "be something you'd mind if I was to touch your asshole while I'm at the duty of suckin' your cock?"

Orkney shook his head.

I felt a pang of regret, of a certain vague loss, as Moe moved forward on the couch and, his lips loose and velvety, took Orkney's cock into his mouth. I could visualize Moe's hand moving around, pressing between Orkney's legs, playing with his balls, and then fingering and caressing his anus, Orkney's wonderful, perfect asshole, sphincter of my staggering joy. And then when Moe reached down and popped the buttons on his pants and his own cock came out, erect, fat, and curving menacingly to one side, I was jolted with the reality of the situation. I could hardly endure even the *thought* of Orkney doing *anything* with it. I almost shouted out for a halt to the performance.

"Don't watch anything too close," Manny whispered. "Not anything *he's* doing anyway. Right now that's a different man over there."

I pulled my eyes away.

Manny had moved to my side.

"And," he said softly, his eyes shining with encouragement, "you're a different man here with me too."

He started running one hand across my back and down my butt to my legs. The other pushed at my bulging crotch.

"You're hard, I can sure feel that," he said, "and that's good. Yeah, baby, that's good." He groped again. "Whatever *else* all this is doing to

43

you, it's sure as hell making you hot."

Well, yes. Of course it was. I am not, after all, blue-and-misty-eyed with purity of heart.

I looked toward the iron bed.

Jack and Jim were both naked now.

On his knees, the mighty ranger's mighty butt, shaggy with tufts of thick black hair, was poised to drive his dick into the tantalizing brown hole offered up by a receptive Jack whose buttocks were opened wide and whose legs were hooked over Jim's massive shoulders. Jim was working at the supple portal with the two middle fingers of his left hand. His other held his own prick, well prepared in a straining stretch, and as hungry and eager a fuck-ram as I've ever seen on any man or beast.

"Hey, bossman," Jack said, "I want to be kissed when you're ready to go up my butt with that big fucker. And I mean kissed hard too."

"Oh you bet, dear boy," Jim replied. "Fucking-a I'll kiss you. I'll kiss *and* fuck you like you ain't never."

"That's what I want to hear, bossman."

Jack put a hand, palm cupped, to his mouth and loaded it with spit.

Then dripping, he slipped his hand between Jim's legs and slopped up the big man's dong, working the loose skin of the ruff up and over and down from the head. And then Jim guided his cock to the hole of mutual desire where, engineering the penetration with two hands, he put the throbbing kernel to the slot and, after just a second or so of resistance, started it on its inward journey, a slick little millimeter at a time. And as Jim went in, Jack's mouth—oh God, his whole face!—was the focus of a thick plaster of Jim's greedily ardent kisses.

Then I too was ready—oh, more than ready—to jump into the boil of this handy pot of passion.

Undoing the buttons of my fly feeling like I was being summoned into the presence of all the lords of fuck and suck of all the millennia, I pulled out my cock, hard and blindly provoked, knowing very well that I was indeed capable of delivering with it even more of the lascivious pleasure of queer love into the very laps of those very lords in their endless, panting wait and, in so doing, fuck down and suck up everything that was ever ordained to be my share.

Jim, moving thickly in a grand dance of butt buggery on the athletic

Jack, cast a fast glance at me, his eyes liquid with pleasure, his lips rosy and wet from kissing, and smirked. Then focusing his full attention on the body, the head, the face—and very likely the soul—of his fuck mate, he moved into the watershed of the jizzshed, celebrating the mysterious prank of sodomy.

"It looks good, doesn't it?" Manny said, his big brown eyes sparkling with lewd enthusiasm. "Oh God, I don't think there's anything more wonderfully depraved looking than two guys stuck together and getting it on fucking butt."

"No," I replied, "I don't suppose there is."

"And that's probably what scares all those preachers out there. At least those who aren't getting a little asshole nookie for themselves now and then. It's how they *think* it'd look to *them*."

"Yes, probably."

"And, God, don't you just love it! All of it!"

"Yes."

Manny smiled and then nodded at the fuckers on the bed. The conclusion drawn there direct, in just a matter of seconds he was stripped to lovely brown skin, an organ of warm, moist, and infinite sensuality.

Manny bent over, opening his buttocks.

"Take it, Clement," he said.

The anus, tight in its rubbery tuck, waited with the hot, rich gifts of pleasure inside.

"Get that dick slicked up and take it, Clement." Manny said.

Spit—the spit of appetite—flowed in my mouth. My tongue rolled in the drench.

"Take it, Clement," Manny said.

Oh, to be sure, lust—the slut born of desire—had me in her grip but still I was snared in just the laciest of doubt.

"For Christ's sake, Clement!" Jim called. "There ain't nothin' ever to surpass that, so get a move on, man. Jesus!"

Never had an exhortation carried a more urgent message.

And so, the spit gathering in my mouth threatening a flood and my cock dumb in anticipation and as stiff as it ever would be, I took in my hand a wad of the magic facilitator and, spreading my cock with a dripping film, moved against Manny's asshole. My cockhead, so clever in its blunt purpose, forced the entry and opened Manny's flesh to my penetration, and as I went into the tight warmth I was immediately under the ancient assault of the honeyed promises of sodomy. Each inward inch of the insertion purred of the thrills awaiting. And when the penetration was complete and I, with a firm grip on Manny's fine shoulders, began the delicious agony of retreat those promises boasted of thrill even headier. Oh God, the indefinite and elusive—but very real—excitation being delivered to me through my penis brought up a sudden and kingly greed, and I wanted every wispy jolt, every jangling caress, every stroking sting that could be gained from a cock—in this case mine—being inserted thus into a cooperative asshole—Manny's. And so, in furthering that aspiration I rolled into the pitch and pull of pelvic thrusts so common and comical in all the males of all history caught up in the bumbling flight toward the promises of love.

"Ho ho. Now that's the ticket there, Clement," Jim called. "And you're lookin' mighty good too."

Of course I wasn't in any *real* need of encouragement but still I liked the message delivered in Jim's few words, and in a few seconds, after I'd really gained a feel for the flow of movement into Manny, I glanced toward Jim and Jack. They, however, were in *no* need of encouragement—or of an audience either. None whatsoever. Their bodies, rolled, folded, tucked, and tied into the soft knot of *their* sexual celebration, were wet with sweat. They kissed and caressed, rubbed and stroked, fingered, felt, and squeezed. There seemed about them, about their cocks mainly—Jack's dancing a stiff sort of stagger between their bellies, Jim's going hell for leather into the hungry bung raised up so eagerly to him—the clutch of a primitive sort of communication, the communication of both selfishness and sharing, the two combined in the simplest way possible.

"When you're ready," Manny said, "I'd like to get on my back."

"I'm ready now," I replied. "I want to kiss you."

"Oh, that'll be nice."

Pulling away from me, Manny rolled into a crouch and then went quickly to his back. His hands taking grips behind his knees, he raised up his legs. Oh hell, I'd seen men in the position before, many times, but with Manny, in his still to me exotic blackness, his undeniable maleness and virility, his beauty, it seemed the most confident and trusting posture ever. And then being regaled, as it were, by his good looking and very hard cock at a high sail above his asshole, I was seized by a pure and purely profane need to love him, to just *love* him, with that love to begin the seeking of its connection through his asshole.

Manny's long arms came up and I went down into them to find his kisses. They, his kisses, were offered to me on his lovely, full lips, darkly hued and now burnished with the perfect luster of lust. I fixed my mouth on his, and in the roll and tongue-ing suck of our common appetite we moved toward the undulating plains that lay soft and indefinite by the turgid sea of anal sex, and there we cavorted for a time in the lush growth and among the wet, sticky flowers of oral gratification.

Manny's mouth was on my neck, his breath a thin rasp in my ear, when he said, "You're an excellent kisser, Clement. Very nice."

I nipped his shoulder and licked the bite.

"And that's nice too," Manny whispered.

Oh dear me, never before had any cock of the walk been cockier in his walk than me.

As I moved my hands to his ankles and my fingers were closing tight, we opened between us another kiss. I waited a few seconds, and then my cock, stiff with deliberate assurance and propelled by my humping hips, regained easily its warm and moist berth in Manny's butt.

"Oh God, Clement," Manny breathed into my mouth. "Christ, push it in deep. Go deep, deep, baby. Go as deep as you fucking can."

Moving into the rhythm of jabbing thrusts and retreating sucks of asshole fucking, we, Manny and me, joined up with the legions of our brothers in the soaring march into the elusive glitter of the tarnished constellation. In the mounting and swooping, climbing and gliding, we enjoyed the mutual fit of our bodies, the accord found in our sloppy trek, and in it we kissed many, many kisses.

Then I dared a glance at the cowhide covered couch.

Moe was on his back, his thick, sturdy legs spread apart where between Orkney's handsome head was bobbing up and down in vigorous cocksucking. His knees on either side of Moe's chest, his long white body arched over Moe's in the perhaps inelegant but effective posture of sixty-nine, Orkney's cock was very much at work in Moe's mouth while his asshole—Orkney's asshole!—was very much the hole of exploration for Moe's fingers, and more than a pair of them too! Moe was pushing into

Orkney, pulling at him, manipulating him, stretching him, *using* him in ways that I never, or thought I never, had, using him in ways that seemed brutal, thickly callous, exploitative, even abusive, and that—and here's the kicker—Orkney in his gobble-gobble-gobble cocksucking actually seemed to relish! My God, Orkney's cock, even if pointing downward, was certainly stiff enough in erection to *demonstrate* beyond any doubt that relish. And you know, in seeing those little dances of degradation being enacted on Orkney and in observing his, well, as I said, his relish for them, the imps of meanness paid me a fast visit wherein I was smacked with a twisted sort of satisfaction in seeing the man of my love so used. And yes, that satisfaction was made even meaner by the fact of our current disconnection. My stomach churned in vindictive joy, my balls tightened in evil delight, my asshole flexed with mindless power as I, enthroned in my cock as never before, experienced in my fucking of Manny the eerie liberation of sexual anarchy.

I looked down at Manny, into the fuckable boy's pretty brown face.

"Oh man, Clement," he whispered, "we're doing all right. We're doing fine. Oh man, I'm going to blow a wad pretty quick."

"I'm not ready," I said.

"That's okay, man. Whenever. Take your time. I like it like that."

"You're sure?"

"Yeah."

His dark eyes bright with passion, Manny heaved his hips higher in the exertions of our copulation, and in doing so his cock, once svelte in ebony elegance, was thrust out like a creature of quiet, secret habits now angrily disturbed. Jerking and jumping, flight seemed its intention, and to thwart that intention I put my fingers around its neck.

"Yeah, man," Manny whispered, "jack that baby off."

My grip imperial, my thrusts zealous, I jacked and fucked, finding nice little places to put quick, wet kisses.

"Oh shit!" Manny cried. "Oh shit, shit, shit!"

Manny's cock, thick in its hot bloat, began the jizzy spume. Time and time again the silvery shots were delivered upon his face and chest while moans of release came from his mouth and shudders wracked his body.

I slowed in the beat of my stroke.

"No, man, don't slow down," Manny said, his eyes closed. "Don't slow down. Go. That fuckhole is yours, baby."

And so, reluctance not even a thought, I continued in the work, kissing and licking and holding close to him, filling out our pocket of passion.

I heard a commotion on the bed.

"Oh bossman!" Jack shouted. "Oh mister bossman, I'm gonna come."

I looked up, ready to watch while I fucked Manny.

"Yep, it's comin', mister bossman!" Jack called. "Oh yeah!"

"Whoa there, kiddo!" Jim shouted. "Hold them horses a sec or two."

Washing Jack's face with another big kiss, Jim plowed on, his butt at a quiver, until, in one last mighty heave of mighty hips, he sank deep into Jack and, with impressive grunts, began shipping out his batch of jizz, the reward for all that gallant labor.

"Oh fuck you, lovely boy!" Jim yelled. "Oh yes, fuck you, lovely boy. Oh yes, fuck you, fuck you, fuck you, and fuck you, you lovely boy."

And then Jack, with one last gentle caress in the effort, brought up his own slap of jizz and spent the glutinous spurts, fabulously abundant, between the two sweaty bellies.

"And there's some hot shit for you, hotshot," he muttered.

Swimming in the drench, the men squirmed and rolled on their bellies. They slipped and slid and wiggled. They bumped and thumped, and Jim farted. They laughed and rolled into a hug, the hug tight, and inside it they played with kisses.

I looked down at Manny. His eyes were closed, his face judiciously expectant as if he were on the last mile into hell.

Moe and Orkney weren't saying much of anything either, their mouths being full of cock, but in its tempo, gusto, and verve their sucking was rising rapidly to a hysteria of mannerly restraint. Putting very apparently everything of their very best efforts into the exertion, from the probing of asshole to the gripping and twisting of nuts, they seemed bound for hours of delicious torture. And then quite suddenly, as if hearing a call from a respected and thunderous deity, Orkney pulled his cock from Moe's mouth and, the thing poised there in stiff splendor, spat out the shots of love, angrily by God, onto Moe's plowboy face.

Moe laughed.

"Always did like a load dumped on my face," he said gathering strings of jizzy-cum on his finger and putting it into his mouth. The cream sucked

49

away, he moved quickly to his knees and, scooting up behind Orkney, began beating off with the slow style of a farmer and all the while rubbing the head of his dick against Orkney's asshole.

"Oh man," Moe murmured, "what a good looking guy you are. Good looking and classy. Such a pissy, classy dude you are. Oh man. Oh man, such a handsome, pissy, classy dude. Oh man. Oh man! Oh man! Yeah! Yeah!" He paused as if awaiting some sort of confirmation, and then, "So now you can take *this* classy shit, dude."

As if a peculiar and precious rite, Moe lay his cockhead on Orkney's bung and, with a soft-toned cooing, anointed the loosened coil with oozes of jizz, the ejaculate luxurious with the sheen of pearls and thicker than axle grease. With viscous design the stuff sagged and dripped and ran down Orkney's anus, off the lovely hole, and into the fleecy golden-red hair on his scrotum.

The two men, their frolic in folly folding into the creamy comfort of satisfaction, slumped down into postures of placid capitulation, their legs and arms thrown this way and that, their cocks, balls, and assholes now but guests invited into the composed moments of afterglow.

But I was not anywhere near composed, nor was I, as a guest or otherwise, being invited into *any* association with that twerpy drip afterglow. No, not me. Not now anyhow. I still had business to attend to.

Manny opened his eyes, smiled, and winked.

"God, Clement," he said, "you've got the staying power of a satyr."

"Are you tired of it?"

"Oh no, baby." He winked again. "But how about this."

I was at the deepest of an inward thrust when Manny tilted his hips upward just a little bit more and while doing so effected a series of quick anal clenches. God, it was terrific. I started to pull back for another go. My cock was alive with the thrilling tingle of the precious trial.

"And how about this." Manny said.

As I pulled back, Manny swung his butt in short little arcs while reapplying the anal clutches. The velvety chute, grown tighter with those clutches, now swayed with rhythmic undulations. My cock—oh God—my cock, my balls, my asshole, my everything! was being wound up and packed into a hot bundle of tender explosives.

"And this," Manny said.

While I continued thrusting and pulling, Manny maintained the clenches and undulations with remarkable control and dexterity, but even *then* he managed to add in a string of upward pushes, jerking and irregular, that met my thrusts coming down. Oh lord, it was an exquisite collision. He worked that performance about three times.

And then it was upon me, the speeding, spewing comet of manhood, the drama before the drench and drip.

Oh dear. Oh lord...

Well, I'm afraid that I have to report that I bellowed in the ejaculation. Oh not the bellowing of rage or impotence, or of fearful injury. No. It was the trumpet of triumph, the thrill of manliness, the anthem of orgasm, the... well, I'm sure you get the idea. Anyhow, after that display, the bellowing, moans, shudders, and so forth, and Manny and I had allowed the slow disengagement of cock from asshole—it was a kind of wilting suck and very pleasant—we settled down on the floor more than ready, but still in a close embrace, to assume a bit of composure for ourselves.

There was a certain silence in the wide room, the silence of satisfaction and even wonder perhaps, and of quiet moments given to hidden speculations and private plans.

And then Jim sprang from his mammoth bed.

"C'mon, Jack," he shouted. "I have a deep hankerin' for some bacon and eggs."

Jim donned an oriental robe and tossed another to Jack and then stomped off toward the kitchen, the magenta garment riding high over his ample rump. Jack followed, completing a procession in his own rustling, silken finery.

Moe stirred on the couch, and Orkney raised his head from between Moe's legs, stretched out his long arms for a moment, and then fell back, going back to his nest in the dense mat of Moe's curly hair, with Moe's balls beneath his chin and Moe's cock resting against his lips.

Manny rubbed my chest, his head on my belly. My hand gripped his shoulder, moved down across his back, stopped above his butt, above the shrine of sodomy, and I remembered, my whole body remembered, the thrill and joy found there.

"Well, I'll be goddamned!" Jim's voice boomed from the kitchen. "Oh my oh my!"

51

"What, Jim?"

"Why, just lookie here, Jack! Eggs and bacon! And, by God, both of the very best quality. Yes sir, we've got some damned fine stuff here."

Orkney grinned at me.

"Hey, Orkney and Clement!" Jim hollered out. "I sure fuckin' thank you guys. Golly, you bet!"

"You're welcome, Jim," Orkney shouted back.

There was an industrious clamor, a steady clank, from the kitchen while the four of us, smugly satisfied in the shimmering languor of receding lust, indulged in the pleasant indirection of post fuck play.

Manny rolled to his side, up on a hip. His slender butt looking precious and perfect and splendid, I went down to it and pressed my face to the slice and raised a buttock and went in with my mouth, my tongue out, to relish the moist and smooth composure of his just fucked asshole. The loose tuck, cleverly elastic even when granting permission, offered small twisted grins in greeting. I kissed it and licked it and lapped it, honoring it for having fucked it.

Manny giggled and pushed his butt back against me.

I felt a grip close on my calf—a strong grip—and I knew that it was Orkney's and that in it he was sending to me a signal of reassurance, of support, of approval. And in that eddy of comfort offered amidst the ever shifting and drifting of standards in the sexual sea, I felt the giddy elation of wonderful decadence, of wholesome debauchery. And feeling so, I gathered up and pulled about my shoulders the lingering remnants of passion, somewhat tattered but still warm, and thus outfitted pressed my face even deeper into the shallow well of love in Manny's asshole and there I sucked and slurped at the sweet nectars seeping out.

"Hey you guys out there! We got bacon fryin' in here!"

"And eggs too!"

"Yeah, and eggs too!"

Indeed.

Always assertive, and now so very staunch in the face of the conflicting propositions being thrust at me, the demanding aroma of frying bacon rolled through the wide room pushing before it the last of the lilt and stagger of ardor and fervor. Even in its leap and dance lust was no match for frying bacon. Alas.

"Somebody's got to be settin' the table," Jim called.

Orkney rose readily to that call to duty, and pulling Moe up by the arm they trooped into the kitchen.

Rolling over and sitting up, Manny scooted to me on his butt and put his hands on my shoulders.

"Oh man, Clement," he said. "That was a fabulous fuck. Everything was fabulous. I figured it would be."

His hand went to my cock indolent in arrogant repose upon my balls. I was stupid with delight at his touch. I swelled with puffs of pride at his tender manipulations.

"Lovely," he murmured, "very lovely. Maybe I'll get to *suck* the juice from it next time." He looked up. "How about it?"

Looking on his handsome brown face, open and earnest, I felt a growing affection beginning to trickle—with a flood threatening—around my heart. And that in turn set the chords of caution to a gentle jangle.

I nodded, slowly but not meaning to.

I felt my face stiffen into an artificial grin.

Manny shook his head.

"Oh, don't worry, Clement," he said, "you're Orkney's fella. I know that."

He pressed a kiss to my cheek.

"C'mon," he whispered, "let's go eat."

We got to our feet and went into the kitchen.

When we sat down to a midday breakfast, Jim's table, in the manner of men robust and simple in their tastes, was a pride and pile of abundance. Bread and muffins and pastries in their packages were flanked by jars of jams and jellies. A tub of margarine, and peanut butter and apple butter, hid among several bags of cookies. A large bowl of fruit cocktail was decorated with sliced bananas and strawberries and strewn with chopped nuts. A tub of Kool-Whip waited nearby. Boxes of corn flakes, Choco-Pops, and puffs of this and that had been put out. Juices in cans and bottles stood in loose formation next to an enormous pot of coffee. But in the middle of the table lay a huge platter of fried eggs, some warmly scorched and all gleaming with a sheen of melted butter. On an adjacent platter thick slices of bacon, glowing a mellow yellow and rich mahogany, were heaped up in voluptuous heartiness with beads of grease running between them. A ton of tater tots were piled into a tureen, steaming like a volcano.

Jim, prim in an apron over his magenta kimono, brought gravy to the table in a deep iron skillet.

"Eat up, you guys," he bid.

And that we did.

Oh yes, we certainly did.

Afterward, when the dishes were almost done, Manny was standing at a window looking out.

"What's that, Jim?" he asked.

"What's what?"

"It looks like some kind of tower. Up there by the rocks."

Jim went to the window to look.

"Oh that," he said. "Yeah. That's an old lookout put up by some desperadoes years and years ago... hell, long before the forestry service ever came up here. And there's more up there than that tower too."

"Like what?" Jack asked.

"Oh, there's some old fences and gates, some barricades and the like, and foundations of what I guess was once cabins and shacks. Quite a few too, and which were, judging by the look of things, destroyed by fire at sometime or other. And all at once too. Then there's a... well, there's what I suppose you could call a dungeon."

"A dungeon!" Jack said.

"Yeah, and behind that there's a cave that goes in quite a ways."

"A cave!" Manny said.

"Yeah, but nothin' exceptional as some caves go. It's just a cave."

"I'd like to take a look," Manny said.

"I would too," Jack said.

"Well, I don't see why not," Jim replied. "You other guys interested in goin' up? Now mind you, it ain't nothin' spectacular as ruins go. It's just kinda nice bein' where men were—men like us maybe—who are all dead and gone now. It's like bein' near them in some way."

Without a whole lot of further discussion it was agreed that we'd all sure like to go up and take a look at whatever it was up there that the desperadoes had found it necessary—or attractive—to build.

And so, getting dressed we set out.

It wasn't a long climb, but it sure was a steep one; the desperadoes had chosen their hideout well.

The trail began right at the back door of the ranger station and climbed up through shelves of rock heavily grown over with chaparral and pitch pine and then crossed the scree beneath the hideout itself. After making a long loop, steep and almost blind through dense sumac, the trail brought us around to the back slope of the hill where, after a scramble over huge rocks, we came suddenly upon a cleft.

Close to ten feet deep, it was also pretty wide.

Jim jumped across, managing an ambitious leap with ease.

He turned.

"Ain't no other way, fellas," he called.

Jack jumped with alacrity and was quickly followed by Orkney, Moe, Manny, and then me.

We continued climbing upward through stones thrown down in rugged natural terraces. The going got tougher as the terraces grew steadily narrower and steeper until they formed a single irregular wall high and sheer enough that getting over it with any ease at all seemed a pretty strenuous undertaking.

"Just follow me, you guys," Jim called, and using little cubbyhole hand and toe holds he led the way around a sharp outcropping and then into a shaft that went off at about forty-five degrees. Navigation required a low crouch.

"Jesus Christ," muttered Moe.

"Stay with it, Moe," Jim sang out gaily. "We're almost there."

"I sure hope so."

And yes indeed, soon enough we came out on the edge of a wide, level clearing.

Smoothly weathered in its dark char, the old lookout tower loomed above angular fortifications and remnants of other ancient construction that somehow denied defeat even while sagging and leaning in abandonment. Rocks crudely squared into blocks—the foundations of the cabins—lay about like weathered gravestones toppled by time.

Moe went stepping among the stones, cautiously as if making careful computations and drawing conclusions.

"Man, this *was* like a little village," he said. "It sure looks like there was more than just a few of those desperado guys here." He laughed.

"Desperado guys and *their* desperado guys."

Orkney fell to his knees and after pulling at the ground for a moment held up a rusty spur. The shank was in a high curve, Spanish style. Moe came over and knelt down to study it with Orkney.

Jim and Jack were bent down together under a cross of burnt timbers sorting though a pile of stones, selecting and polishing certain treasures on their thighs.

I sat down on a bench of heavy planks, worn a satin-like gray from years of exposure, and gazed across a carpet of trees to the canyon, the river deep within. Our place, Orkney's and mine, was way off and hidden behind the cliff, but I could see it well in my mind's eye, and I wondered if this now lonely and abandoned stronghold of those 'desperadoes' had ever been as important to them as our place was to Orkney and me. I was suddenly washed with a very acute reminder of how important home and Orkney—the two almost one—were to me, and how I would, because I could do no other, protect them with every ounce of my strength and to my last breath. There was a chill of threat in the thought that maybe this new freedom we were designing, so scary and yet so inviting, was doing less in strengthening our bonds and more in posing a subtle jeopardy.

"Here's the dungeon," Manny called from a distance away, across the clearing and up near the boulders. "Come and check it out, you guys."

Jim looked my way.

"That's about the most inquisitive young fella ever," he said shaking his head. "I'd've shown him where it was soon enough."

I moved toward the boulders, toward Manny.

Orkney and Moe followed

Manny was down in a squat and peering into a low dark fissure between two massive slabs of stone, those laid down by glaciers long, long ago. But built up around that basic—and natural—structure were stones placed by the hands of creatures fully intent on fashioning for themselves a chamber of solid strength.

And it was a good job too.

The stones, some angular and wide and thick, others narrow and thin, were fitted together with remarkable precision. Quite clearly it was not something done in the haste of a weekend.

Orkney was studying the work closely.

"I don't think this was done by any desperadoes," he said. "More likely it's the work of Indians, and many, many years—probably hundreds—before any white men ever showed up." Manny popped a short laugh. "But you can sure bet they used it when they did."

"No doubt," Orkney agreed.

"I'm going in," Manny said and slipped through the fissure.

"Me too," Moe said and followed.

Orkney shrugged and, bending down, entered the hole.

And me?

Well, knowing what you know up to this point, wouldn't you?

Inside was the dim light of a bad dream, the shadowy nothingness of the one worst fear made somehow real and, being so, shrouded in eerie, timeless waiting. The light came down from a small hole high up: ventilation. The walls, though jagged and rough with fitted stonework, were nearly perpendicular and allowed sufficient room for about a half dozen men engaged in reasonably active pursuits.

And what if...

And what if not those, those reasonably active pursuits?

"Boy oh boy, it looks like they could've kept maybe ten guys chained up in here," Manny said, moving around.

To which Moe observed, "I wonder why they'd want to do that. I don't think desperadoes kept prisoners."

"We don't know, Moe, that they actually did," Orkney said.

"Oh they did all right," Manny said from a corner. "Look. Here's a chain hanging from the wall, and there's an iron cuff on it. And here's another one. And another."

"Indians or desperadoes," I said, "they certainly didn't share nice little picnics in here."

Manny went to a squat with his back to the wall, his arms spread wide, his hands gripping the ancient chains. He in his fine countenance, his slender and excellent body glowing with the health born of African resilience and American strength, seemed a boy playing at the horrors of his elders while in fact himself quite innocent of their depravity. Seeing him, youthful and spotless, amusing himself thus I was suddenly seized by an awful desire to witness him in degradation. I felt churns of lust run my body while serpents of greed twined about my arms and legs. My shorts, my baggy hiking shorts, went forward at the push of an erection, an erection of erotic defiance. I saw me as a potential enslaver eagerly willing.

No! I thought. No, not me! That's not me! No, that's not the real me wishing to see thrown upon this fine and lovely young man the thick and stiffly savage robes of degradation. No!

"How'd you like to see me chained up like this, Clement?" Manny said. "Every day."

"No. Not... not... " I stammered. "Well, no... Not... "

"Maybe not every day," Moe said. "But for right now I'd say it looks a pretty good proposition. The man's getting a hard on."

"I can see that," Manny said.

I put my hand down to my fly.

"Pull it out, Clement," Manny said. "Pull it out and let me watch you work it hard. Get it real hard like you can and jack off while I watch. Make me want it."

Manny gazed upon me in cunning expectation, as if upon an oppressor of charming capabilities. The serpents on me, in me, and of me, turned and squeezed, rolled and twisted, and I brought out my erection, brought it out in its hot preen, in its hefty urge, in its hugely fabulous capacity.

"Well Jesus Christ, man," Moe said, "there it is right there, and it's a super stiff stiff too."

"Come closer, Clement," Manny whispered, "Come closer and stick it in my mouth and let me suck it."

In a staggering step, I moved toward Manny, toward his mouth, toward his body, toward *him* in all his profane and godly beauty.

I could feel his breath on my cockhead.

It came in short, hot bursts.

I thrust my hips forward.

I felt the brush of his warm, soft lips.

"Atta boy," Moe murmured.

I thrust again.

In.

"Atta boy."

I thrust again and the lips closed.

"Oh yeah, atta boy," Moe murmured again. "Oh man."

Moe's fingers closed about my cock and then went down and around the root and urged me deeper into Manny's mouth, the fit and the desire the same. Moe stroked and squeezed in the wet pushing and pulling, giving succor in advancing this new expedition into our queer mission of suck.

"Yeah, Manny," Moe whispered, "fuckin' suck dick, baby."

Manny's mouth the wettest and hottest of wet hot heavens, I pushed in going for the slick grip of his throat.

Orkney, standing at my back, put his arms across my chest and bent and pressed his face to my neck. His bites there, small and cat-like, sent little darts of lust dancing throughout my body in exquisite jabs of mindless thrill, of shooting passion built in sweet pain.

"Shall I fuck you, Clement?" he said.

I nodded, and turning my head I opened my mouth soliciting his kiss.

"Fuck me, Orkney," I whispered against his lips.

I could feel the prod of hard male meat at my asshole, the stiff organ seeking to open the tacky tuck, to get into it, and to bring up the fast push of full penetration.

"Fuck me, Orkney."

Moe's fingers danced nimbly about, eager in assistance.

"It's slick we need here," he muttered, and gathering spit into his hand he said, "And, by God, it's slick we got."

The spit spread, Orkney's cock came against my asshole as an army of one. Its stiffness was without rival, its length heroic, its thrust vigorous and bold. I received it as the king of lands vast and rich and ready to go under the plow.

Under the plow indeed.

Bending my knees, tilting my hips, and pushing back my butt, I took Orkney's cock all the way up my ass just as Manny took mine all the way down his throat. In the shadowy elegance of a sleek depravity, as if wearing gowns of sheer finery and hung with jewelry of exhibition, I entered again into the steamy chambers of butt fucking and cock sucking but with, oh lord, in this particular case both butt and cock being mine. Posed on the threshold of a queer nirvana, I was enthralled by the possibilities of queerdom, both those in aroused abstraction and those—mine—in the sweaty reality of the very moment.

"By God's indulgence, Clement, you do have a way of gettin' yourself into some juicy fixes."

I looked over my shoulder.

Jim, beaming like a bishop, stood just inside the dungeon entrance, and Jack stood right behind him.

"You're all lookin' just peachy, fellas," Jim said and turned. "What's your thought on the matter, Jack?"

"Good."

"That's swell," Jim replied. "So what say you and me get in on it."

"Yeah."

Jim flipped the clasp on his khaki shorts, they fell to the ground, and he stepped out, his cock stiffening up to its full potential in seconds. Jack's peter was hard coming out of his Levi cutoffs. He was stripped to skin in no time at all.

"My oh my, fellas," Jim said taking mincing steps toward Moe, "what on earth shall we do here."

His eye brows raised in lecherous expectation, he gazed on us one from the other. Enacting as I was the fornication of all fortune—being humped in asshole while humping in mouth—I felt my comment be best made in silence. Orkney however wasn't so reticent.

"By God's greasy gonads, Jim," he sang out, "Moe's is a sweet bung in a handsome bum. Get yourself a piece of that."

"That's a good thought there, Orkney," Jim agreed. "Good thought. Now if I was to get myself hooked up in somethin' like ole Clement's got here, maybe I... "

The crafty old ranger bent low in front of Jack presenting point blank his big furry butt in invitation to enjoy a nice hot fling in sodomy. Jack wasn't lost to the idea for, indeed, no sooner had Jim assumed the position did Jack have his hands on the massive buttocks, the crease spread open, and his cock put firmly against the Jim's pretty pink slot. Summoning up a good wad of spit, Jack wrapped his cock in the sloppy helper and, with nary a sigh, shoved in.

"Umph," Jim grunted. "That's good. Oh that's good." He pushed back against Jack a few times, getting the fit, and then stood up.

"C'mere, Moe," he said.

Moe moved to Jim, his cock pulled up nicely in a staunch erection.

Jim took a grip on it. "Nice tool, boy."

Moe took a grip on Jim's. "This is nice too."

"Nice enough to go up your butt?"

"You bet."

"Okay, bend over."

"Go get it, Jim," Orkney said plowing into me while I pumped into Manny. Working together, Jim and Jack gathered up more than enough spit to slop up hole and cock alike for this new go at the old game of buggery. And then glistening with spit applied to it in unholy enthusiasm, Jim put his cock to Moe's asshole and pushed in as Jack pushed into him.

Jesus Christ, all the high wire tortures of our queer ecstasy were thrown down to us in that lonely, dim hole in a rock where we, in a group and each unto himself, grabbed hold for yet another mad swing at the impossible dream.

Manny, ever diligent in his sucking, took my scrotum in hand and with the most artful finesse began a steady manipulation, pulling and squeezing, a twist and a tug here and there, that skated from time to time on the fringes of pain, a pain of provocative caprice. With Orkney's first-rate plugging of my butthole, a couple of the pirouettes of nuance there being a pouncing way of getting at my prostate and some deft movements done with his cockhead inside the rim.

"Neat, huh, Clement?" Jim said, his mouth wet and loose in an ingratiating smile, his dark, glassy eyes hooded. "Oh Jesus, I'm flyin' as high as heaven's ever gonna let me what with these two lovely lads workin' me over the way they are. Shit, I could be shipped to hell tomorra and I'd still be happy."

"You ain't goin' to hell, bossman," Jack said.

"Just a manner of speakin', Jack. Keep on fuckin', kiddo."

"And here comes hell now," I shouted, "hot from the hinges."

Success in Manny and Orkney's work delivered to me an ejaculatory orgasm with the excruciating brilliance of pain. With the soaring might of a demented angel I blasted the buttons off God's butt and heaved the stuff, wired with the twists of torture its supposed to have, into Manny's mouth, into his throat. He gagged, but swallowed, and then remained still, keen to the end in his dedication. In my dizzy whirl, I could feel the contractions of the spew in my cock, in the root of my cock, in my nuts, and in my asshole stretched as it was around Orkney's big Scottish prick.

"I can feel that, Clement," Orkney said running his rod into me with steady measure.

I flexed my anal muscles, seeking in the flexing to own Orkney's cock.

"How's that," I croaked.

"Fab, luv."

I flexed again. "And that?"

"Oh that's fab too."

And so I flexed again, and again, and again.

"That's all fab too, luv."

Then Manny stood up.

"Now squat down a little, Clement," Orkney ordered.

I squatted down and Manny's cock, stiffer than a preacher's starched shirt, slapped at my mouth.

"Suck Manny off, Clement," Orkney said. "Get that boy's cum."

And now I sucked being fucked. My cock, dripping and gone limp and long, hung against my leg.

"Hey, Clement," Jim called gaily, "ain't we just like two peas in a pod? Well, I mean kinda like. Jesus Christ, this is swell. I could fuck like this for fuckin' forever. Well, almost."

"I'm not gonna last forever, Jim," Moe said. "Not even almost, I don't think."

Jack, busy, busy Jack, moaned as if in deep distress, then muttered, "Whatever the fuck forever is, this is it." I heard the wet smack of flesh to flesh, the pull and farty sucking of fast, frantic thrusts. "Oh yeah, man," Jack groaned, "this is the last day of fuckin' forever"—he gasped—"right now and, hey bossman, I got some"—and he gasped again—"jizz squirts comin' up to help you out." I heard the throttled cry, the stifled sob, the moaning trial of orgasm. And after another groan, another gasp I heard, "Now, bossman! And it's my best fuck and you got it up your butt."

"Oh Jack, my dear boy. Oh Jack! Oh Jack!"

Moe said, "Hey, Mister Ranger Man, it's *me* you're fuckin'."

"Oh Jesus Christ, Moe! Oh Jesus Christ, Jack! Oh Moe! Oh Jack!"

"Oh for Christ's sake, you guys!" Manny shouted, "the dude's about to come! Can't you tell?"

"Shit yeah!" Moe shouted. "And me too!"

Planning to get in the play, I redoubled my efforts in sucking Manny. He put his hands on the back of my head and, bending down, whispered, "And me too, baby. In a minute."

"Whoopee!" Jim yelled. "This Moe dong is hard and hot. Oh boy."

"Squeeze my nuts," Moe said.

"I'm squeezin' nuts," Jim replied. "Oh yeah, I'm squeezin' nuts and. fuckin' butt."

"Here come the fuckin' train!" Moe shouted, the shout quickly lost in the rolling anguish of ejaculation.

"Whoopee!" Jim yelled. "Man oh man! Man *oh* man, and what a fuckin' load! Man oh fuckin' man!" Then Jim grunted, a slow, low grunting deep and personal. "And now, Moe," he muttered, "here's a little something to carry in your caboose."

Grabbing my ears, Manny pulled himself into me, his cock into me, the thick, stiff thing going into my throat where, as I waited forever expecting to die any minute, he brought up his jizz-jazz payoff and pumped it down, deep into my guts. After the passing of the tremors through Manny's body, I played my tongue around the head of his cock lapping and pushing at the hole of the jizzy milk.

Oh Lord.

Somebody coughed, somebody spit, and then, like leaves falling from trees in the winds of autumn change, we disengaged, separated, and rearranged ourselves talking softly in short utterances, and giggling now and then.

"So where's the cave, Jim?" Manny said, all buttoned up.

"Back there behind that outcropping. It's all right for a little ways, but then you have to go through a real tight place to a drop of maybe eight, ten feet. After that though it's a clear shot to the spring."

"How far altogether?" Moe asked.

"Not more'n two hundred yards," Jim replied. "Maybe two hundred fifty tops."

"Let's go," Manny said.

"This ain't no tourist attraction, kiddo," Jim advised. "It's darker'n hell in there."

"I've got a flashlight," Manny responded.

"Oh hell," Moe said, "let's go in."

"Right," Jack agreed.

"We can have us a little bath at the spring," Jim said.

"That's good enough for me," Orkney said.

"Now if everybody stays real close together," Manny said, "we'll be okay.

He didn't have to tell me that. Caves never have been places I'd go out of my way to visit, but being with the group through thick or thin—for the present at least—I took my place in the middle of our single file as we set off into the inner chamber of the rocky mountain.

It wasn't a bad go. No, not bad at all. Manny was a good guide. As he went forward into an almost immediate darkness he would play about his really rather feeble light and describe what we could expect to encounter as we groped along one behind the other. Moe and Jack maintained a steady stream of chatter, and Jim made a comment now and then, but Orkney and me were pretty much silent.

The toughest part was getting down the shaft Jim had mentioned. The drop was more than eight or ten feet. It was closer to fifteen. But there were several foot and hand holds to use here and there, and each with the assistance of the others down with just a few falls, bumps, and thumps.

"Is everybody okay?" Manny called out, his voice eerily resonant in the black void.

"We're all right," Moe said.

"Yeah. We're okay."

The trek out was the longest part but the easiest, probably because we were gaining in confidence. But anyway, soon enough we came out into daylight under a long, low overhang of an outcropping. We crept along a narrow ledge for a short distance, and then after coming around an enormous boulder entered into a shallow grotto, and the spring.

"This is wonderful Jim," Orkney said.

And wonderful it was.

The spring seemed to surface between stones higher up and from there the water seeped, dripped, and trickled down the rocks until it was collected in several troughs that carried it to a large wooden tub. An ancient mountain beech, probably fifty feet high, stood above, its swooping branches and twisted roots seeming to be the mainstay in holding everything together. Several smaller trees, canyon redbud and variegated aspen, grew in clusters, their lacy leaves giving shade and protection to rock fern, nightshade lily, and Indian wampum bush.

"That's the bath, fellas," Jim said pointing to the tub. "It took me, six other guys, and a team of mules to lug that son of a bitch up here, so you'd better enjoy it. I've heard it said though, that the water's a mite chilly."

Well, we all stripped down and headed for the tub and, yes, soon discovered that the water was indeed 'a mite chilly'. But not enough to prevent several minutes of spirited splashing and a little rough-housing. Then one by one we climbed out to find the warmth of the afternoon sun on a deck built into a steep hillside of rocks grown over with cascading vines and delicate conifers.

Manny was the last to leave the tub. His sleek body, his rich color even richer from the cool water, seemed the incarnation of some lovely creature of leafy, rocky grottoes, a creature widely rumored but not often seen.

He lay down, falling into an indolent sprawl, his body half in dappled sunlight, and then came up on an elbow.

"God, Jim," he said," we sure have to thank you for bringing us up here."

"It's my pleasure, Manny," Jim said, "though it ain't near thank you enough for all them other real pleasant things you—and I mean all of you guys—have done for, with, and to me. Land sakes, I ain't never had such a time. Well, not in recent memory anyway."

I looked at Manny, and then at Moe and Jack, wanting to say something as gracious—and direct—as Jim, but I couldn't. Not that I wouldn't; I just knew I couldn't because it wouldn't sound the same.

"How's the best way to get back down to the bridge," Moe asked. "We got our gear stashed down there."

"It's only a quarter mile or so to the station," Jim said. "Or there's a trail, though not a very clear one, that goes along the creek. It takes you down to the river. It comes out upstream of the bridge."

"I think that's what we'll do," Manny said. "Okay, Moe? Jack?"

Moe and Jack both agreed that that would be okay.

"Jesus," Manny said, "this is so perfect I hate to leave."

"Aye," Orkney said softly.

But after about another quarter hour in the sun, the shadow of the ridge working up toward us, a stir crept into our reverie and people began to

65

move. We dressed and then stood around in a loose knot, looking at one another but not wanting to look.

"It was great, bossman," Jack said extending a hand to Jim.

"You can say that again, kiddo. You can climb into my bed anytime."

Well, that exchange started the ball rolling. We all said things, this and that things, as we got ready to separate. Manny and I shook hands, and started to embrace, but we didn't. Moe threw a playful punch at Orkney's midsection and missed, and then, laughing, took a solid one from Orkney.

"Just remember, you guys," Jim said leading the way to the trail down into the canyon. "Always follow water because water always flows down hill, and because it does it'll always get you somewhere. Maybe not always where you want to go but it'll get you somewhere."

"Got it, Jim," Manny said and turned away and started down, went around a thicket of laurel and was soon gone from sight.

Jack and Moe followed.

"Fine young fellas," Jim said, "but it wouldn't do to run into the likes of them too often. I'm plumb tuckered out."

"You're one hell of a highland stud, Jim," Orkney said.

"Why thank you, Orkney," Jim replied, a certain swagger in his hips.

"Now, c'mon you guys," he said, "let's hightail it back to the station. I'm goin' into town tonight. Ole Bub said he might be comin' over from Vegas. He ain't no spring chicken but he can still cut the mustard. So to speak, that is"

And hightail it we did.

Fast.

Back at the station and after a few words of parting, Orkney and me got into the flatbed and started up to our place. We drove along in silence for a while, the canyon below now deep in dark shadows.

"How do you feel, Clement?"

"Okay."

"I'm not asking after your health."

"I know that. I feel okay. Different, but okay. You?"

"I feel different too. Better."

We turned up the road, narrow and rocky, to our place, the house in its weathered gray glowing with a reassuring permanence in the last golden light of the sun.

We put the truck in the garage and walking through the garden we stopped to pick some snap beans and pull up a few beets. We found an eggplant hidden in the tangle of squash vines.

Orkney went down into the smokehouse and brought up a couple of ham hocks.

"How about hocks and lima beans for dinner?" he said.

"Good enough. Shall I make cornbread or biscuits?"

"Cornbread. Do it with the chilies and onions. I like that."

And so we went into the house—our house—and set about the tasks and pleasures that keep our lives moving on the forward course toward an unknown future.

A little later, the hocks and beans at a low simmer on the stove, I stood at the door looking at the cliff, now black and formless in its crags and faces. I wondered where Manny, Moe, and Jack might be.

Orkney came and put his across my shoulders.

"You're thinking about them, aren't you," he said.

"Yes."

Orkney sighed. "Jim was right. I'm not so tuckered out, but it wouldn't do to run into the likes of them too often."

"Why?" I asked, a small chill running my neck.

"Oh I suppose it's this modest life I'm growing so partial to. It seems that maybe that sort of thing—and, mind you, I'm not changing my mind about it, not entirely—brings in a kind of disruption that isn't needed. Not really."

"I see."

I gazed on Orkney's handsome face.

He smiled and said, "Give me time, Clement."

"You can have all the time you want or need, Orkney. I just hope that I'll always be included."

The next day Orkney and I drove into town.

Jim Fleetwood's pickup was parked under the trees at the side of The Happy Scouts Motel.

We went on up the street and stopped in front of the Miracle Sheen Auto Painting and Fine Upholstery Shop.

We sat for a few minutes.

I looked at Orkney.

67

"Red?" I said.

"Or green."

"Maybe we should buy a new truck instead."

"Maybe."

I shrugged. "I know this one's kind of old, but it runs."

Orkney nodded.

"And good too," he said.

Orkney put his hand on my knee, and then ran it up my leg. I felt that pleasure, but not quite so precarious now.

"Oh, come on, Clement," Orkney said, "let's go home."

"Yeah, let's go home."

TWO

STACE AND FILLMORE

There were two of them.

Two really beautiful, masculine men.

Oh God, they were gorgeous. The one was massive, sculpted, direct; the other slender, elegant, poised.

Their names were Stace and Fillmore.

They were cousins I think. Or maybe even half-brothers. I never really knew for sure, but that didn't matter. Nothing mattered then except that I thought they were the two most beautiful men on earth—I could have worshipped the dirt, *and* the shit, on their boots—and *they* didn't even know that I existed. Well, I mean other than the kid who, since being shipped to that farm in eastern Arkansas, worked at helping them slop all those damned hogs and do other farm stuff.

I can't in all honesty say that I *loved* any of that but I was with them, well, at least some of the time. But they were *always* together. Stace, the big man, seemed to have his hands on Fillmore somewhere almost all the time. He'd hang onto his belt, run his hands across his shoulders, mess with his hair, slap at his butt.

And, like I said, almost all the time!

Anyway, this aunt of mine and her snotty new husband (a *permanent* student at the Celestial Rhapsody Theological Institute of Tulsa) had shipped me to the country so as to be rid of me for as long as possible, maybe permanently if I'd do them a favor and just die. Since my mother had and my father'd taken a powder a little later and there wasn't any money to be had in keeping me (just a shell of some obscure family duty impossible to ignore had saved me from Lane Hall) I'd been bumped around in the status of an unwanted but not unruly boy until this aunt finally took me in. Well anyhow, whatever the damned circumstances, the new husband—the bible belter—was more than a little pissed off with having *me* under *his* new roof, and so he fixed it that they made arrangements to ship me off to the country roads of Arkansas with nothing but a suitcase with what few clothes I had and my books.

I didn't even have shit-kicking boots.

But all that stuff isn't what I'm *really* talking about here.

Who cares.

I'm talking about those two beautiful men.

I'm talking about Stace and Fillmore.

Even if they didn't know *I* existed, I sure knew *they* did. Boy, did I ever! I can't count the jackoff hours I spent thinking about them. Oh God, out there in the woods I'd strip down naked and pretend I carried the sleek physique of Fillmore, the younger one, on my gawky bones, while Stace, the powerhouse, would do hazy *things* to us, to Fillmore and me, things *against* us, *ideas* of things I couldn't even *begin* to define but *knew* existed. With my hot imagination at work, whatever the wheels of the fantasy, it wouldn't take long and there I'd be on my back with my legs pushed against some damned tree and my butt up high offering my asshole to *somebody* for *something*. With my peter—so neatly circumcised—inches, oh God, *miles,* from my mouth, and longing to suck it, I'd jack off, sometimes until my neck hurt, all the while entertaining vague daydreams of what it would be like if my two cousins—as I liked to think them—were to come along and find me in such a pose. A tight scuffle? A scolding? A whipping maybe? Some nasty little tortures? And *then* tears and holding and gentle comfort? And kisses? Kisses! Oh God! *and what else*! Well, after a little while the ignorant but energetic contemplation of the unknown *and* that determined *manual* effort would finally overwhelm and I'd be grabbed again by the crazy dying. I'd watch with what I *knew* was a sinful joy as the slitted lips above would open and throw out the hot stuff, the jizzy-juice, onto my face and into my mouth. *It*, that unbelievably intense moment of brilliant light and excruciating ecstasy, was my one precious, private miracle and I could only wish that it would last forever. But of course it never did. With the jizz splattered on my face and slapped into my mouth, my tongue seeking out errant drops (I was an intuitively if quietly perverted little devil), I would slump into the dusty grass, naked and sticky and, once again, very much alone.

Well damn.

And then suddenly much to my surprise all that, and other things as well, changed.

At least for that summer.

I was standing on the bridge gazing down into the sluggish green water wondering in ignorant adolescent abstraction if I'd ever really *go* anyplace—well, shit, just *any* place other than a damned hog farm in Arkansas—when someone grabbed me about the waist, hoisted me about a foot above the rickety railing, and dangled me there like a toy.

"I'm gonna throw you in, boy."

Somehow expecting—or perhaps more like wistfully hoping for—someone to seize me so, instead of struggling I just sagged, went limp. My feet were soon back on the deck. Big firm hands in a masculine grip turned me by my narrow shoulders.

It was Fillmore.

"God, kid," he said in his song of a tenor voice, "I sure as hell didn't mean to scare you none."

His clear, untroubled blue eyes, innocent to the depth of his country soul, looked into mine. If it hadn't been for the railing I'd have fallen over, right into the creek.

I opened my mouth to speak, but for my life I couldn't think of a thing to say.

"Jesus, are you all right, kid?"

I nodded.

Fillmore's solicitous concern seemed to speed away just as fast as it had arrived. He looked down at the water, his hands thrust into his back pockets, his butt square under his hips, his feet apart, his shoulders pitched forward.

"I been huntin' for Stace," he said moving his gaze from the creek and off through the trees. "You ain't seen him, have you?"

71

I shook my head.

"That big galoot," Fillmore said, "I wonder just where the hell he could be. Damn, now where do you s'pose he could be?"

Commenting on all *that* was way beyond me.

And then with a booted foot propped on the lower rail and a firm, denim-clad thigh so close I could have leaned on it, I was compelled, made breathless, by the nearness of *him*, and all I could do was stand there and stare, without a smidgen of real hope, at his crotch. Incredibly full and *thrusting* with masculinity, I remember being fascinated by the offhand way the metal buttons managed to hold it all together. It was the mightiest arrangement of simplicity I'd ever seen.

"Hey there!" Fillmore said. "What you lookin' at, boy?"

I peered up into his face and saw, not wrath there, but a gentle, encouraging smile. He moved his hand to the back of my neck. In another moment he pulled me to him, my face nuzzling against his chest. He smelled of private places and personal things. My thoughts were of underwear and socks and fingers put certain places at night. My hand crept to his waist and dared to find a hold on his belt that was oh! so achingly close to the promised land. Wrapped in the most elusive warmth *and* my pup of passion yelping for attention, I could have stayed that way forever.

"By God," Fillmore said, "I just thought of somethin'. Yeah. I think I know where that ole Stace is."

Fillmore's arms were lifted from me, and I was alone again.

A few paces away Fillmore stopped and turned.

"Well, kid, c'mon now."

I hurried toward him.

At the end of the bridge a huge cottonwood tree stood among granite boulders, and a narrow trail wound down through those rocks and came to an end under the bridge itself. I followed this wonderful man down there even though I knew the way quite well by myself.

Darker and cooler than outside and more than a little sinister—to a thirteen year old boy at least—I'd always imagined it to be, with enticing chills, a place of the forbidden, a dangerous stage set for nasty things. It smelled of old wood, dry weeds, and dust.

"Aha! You got him, Fillmore."

"Yeah, I did."

"And you did good, honey."

Deeper amongst shadowy rocks I could see Stace sitting on a shallow outcropping. His legs crossed like a primitive potentate, he was completely naked. Always massive in musculature and bulk, he presence was now nearly overwhelming. I was enchanted but I still might have fled had it not been for Fillmore's softly restraining hand on my shoulder.

"Pull his pants down," Stace said, getting up on one knee. "I want to take a look at that pretty little butt of his."

"Go easy, Stace."

"Dammit, I will!"

I was dizzy.

I was scared.

I wanted to run, to hide.

And I wanted also to do as I was told. Most of all, and for reasons I couldn't understand, I wanted so much to do just that.

Turning me as if for inspection, Fillmore stripped my shorts to my ankles and had my shirt off in seconds. Stace came closer. He was distorted, in my limited experience, by an enormous bulk that I suddenly realized was a fully erected, man-sized penis. Jesus Christ, it was a monument! Aghast and yet fascinated far beyond redemption, and feeling so strangely right in that gloomy place, I wanted to fall on my knees and admire it, caress it, worship it, and in that worship put my mouth on it.

I didn't *think* about it. I just knew that I *had* to do it.

Then Stace was at my back, feeling and stroking my butt, humming to himself and grunting.

"Oh you juicy little squirt," he said. "I been lookin' at you ever since you first showed up here."

Fillmore put his hand on top of my head as if meant in some sort of reassuring gesture. Although I certainly liked it, the need in me was not crucial. For being in the hands of these two men a kind of faith came down to me and I knew that I was going to go somewhere at last, to a place I didn't even understand but even with that I was more than glad—I was elated!—to be on the journey. I knew as instinctively as a kid knows anything that I would not be harmed. It was in that new faith that I allowed myself to be lowered to the polished stone beneath my feet. My legs were raised high, and I was rolled far up on my back to my shoulders. Floating

73

dreamily above my face my cock and balls seemed strangely new to me as this adventure was, quite incredibly, opening all around me almost as in those hot fantasies. Expecting so much without knowing what to expect, I wanted only, and without question, to be of, for, and with these men.

"He's young, Stace. So, Jesus, you better go easy on 'im."

"Aw shit, I ain't some weirdo, y'know. I just want to look at his puddin' hole before anything gets done to it."

"Go easy, Stace. I ain't sayin' it but once."

"Then, goddammit, I done heard you once."

"Okay."

Stace pressed a finger on the spot.

Oh Christ, the thrill of it! The touch on that extra special part of me by another—not me!—sent ripples of the keenest pleasure out from its center and into my belly, sending out the impatient call for more of the same, *much* more of the same. My cheeks wide, my pelvis in a dancing squirm upward, I watched above as Fillmore stripped off his clothes, revealing him to be every inch the perfect man I knew him to be, longed to be myself, and yearned to be for. I was in the dreamiest enchantment, lost in the folds of realized fantasy.

Then the probing at me gave way to a hot, moist lapping, a scrubbing by an angel of greed then new to me but immediately adored. Being but the opening pages of ensuing chapters, these new acts and arts were visited on me with care and I accepted them willingly, the thought of resistance never even occurring to me. There was no need of explanations, of reasons, of evasions. It was done and I conceded it, aided in it, because it felt right. I knew that it was right. It was, I knew then as well as now, my mode, my avenue, my conduit to humanity and, thus, back to me and a possibility of completion.

And so, my small, thin frame bent to his use, Stace sucked and licked and lapped at my asshole. I felt giddy in a silly, girlish way, and yet quite old, as if I'd been asked into a shelter of secrets dusty with silence.

And then, my ankles loose in the grips of his huge fists, Stace lay me down into a sprawl, open and available, like new goods.

"This kid's ready, Fillmore. You go on him first since it was you that brung him down."

Stace sat back on his haunches.

74

My legs came down and my new friend Fillmore, resplendent in an elegant erection, came astraddle my chest and put his penis to my lips. The inclination possibly, oh God, no doubt there always, the actual fact now at hand, I took in the magnificent orb. How splendid that sleek, functional thing fit! I then tested the orifice with my tongue. As a boy I was more than casually acquainted with piss, but the connection at that very moment eluded me because those dim symbolisms were still busy finding hooks to hang on, but the general gist of the scheme, if you will, was firmly in place and I knew it. I watched Fillmore watching me in this experimentation. Wanting so much to please him, when he began the drive through my mouth toward my throat, I took it as it was pushed at me. Bigger than anything I'd ever put into my mouth before, I handled it with my best effort and in quiet determination until I knew that I could take no more. Tears of exertion filled my eyes but lascivious joy filled my heart, filled it nigh to bursting for I'd made a start even though I still didn't fully comprehend the nature of the journey.

"You ain't gonna come off in him like that, are you?" Stace said
"We gotta be careful."

"Hell, we got us some sweet stuff here, Fillmore. This ain't somethin' we get everyday, y'know."

Stace was on his massive knees beside us, working one fist upon that stupendous cock. The other manipulated the nipples on his epic chest. Reaching out I took the big man's balls in hand. So delicate in concept, so potent in action, they were now warm, velvety, and friendly in my grip.

I smiled upward.

Stace popped a short, quick laugh.

"Oh shit, Fillmore," he said, his voice a rolling gloat, "didn't I tell you this kid'd be one hot fuckin' pistola! Oh goddammit!"

Fillmore maintained his assault against my face. The comfort of the penetration growing as the experience itself moved away from novelty and toward a conclusive mission, he became less restrained in his thrusts, more urgent, more emphatic in the assertion of his masculine prerogative. The man seemed about to embark on a fantastic flight and I was sure he was going to take me along.

And then he stopped.

I looked up into his eyes.

"No, not yet," he said softly, denying my mouth him. "Not yet, my hungry boy-man."

So involved had I been with the overwhelming genital presences of the two giants, I had dismissed my own to the dim shadows where lurk those who look on, but that was jarringly changed when Fillmore moved lower, raised my legs up to his shoulders and took my cock into his mouth.

God, I could have pissed with ecstasy!

With Fillmore working, I'm sure, only a few of all the miracles he had to bring a boy to the very brink of shooting for the stars, I was in an emotional and physical turmoil being, as I was, bathed in his attention. In that turmoil, I was so caught up in the thrill of the call, the summons to be his in whatever way he wanted me to be, that the manner or method of that possession wasn't even important. It was far more than enough that it was my cock he had implanted in his mouth, that it was my asshole that he fingered as he sucked, that it was my scrotum that he held tight as he pulled downward inching me ever closer to the spewing that his sucking was demanding of me. It was me, just me, that he wanted, and I was owned in the most exquisite way. The actual *purchase*, however, was looming nearer and nearer with each new leap from pinnacle to peak in that virgin quest for freedom.

Oh God, it was exquisite!

You can't expect much articulation from a confused adolescent but the yen was there for the freedom—that ancient, battered bulwark of human dignity—to be one's self, freedom long hidden from realization so deep in old, pernicious myth and mangled and trod upon by those charged with its administration that its very recognition is often—oh goddammit!—lost in ignorant, cowed, frightened inertia.

I felt all that, I suppose, but I couldn't have said it. I wouldn't have even if I could. And so I held closely to Fillmore in whatever way I could, mounting, receding, and mounting again to meet that shimmering, asshole holy goal.

Stace rose up.

"I gotta fuck," he announced.

Effecting mighty pelvic thrusts and gazing upon me, the meat he really wanted, he was formidable but not fearsome.

"Oh Fillmore," he moaned, "oh God, I gotta fuck."

In his fist his fat cock was singing a flat, silent song of lechery.

Fillmore shook his head.

"Well, Stace," he said, "you're gonna have to fuck me 'cause you sure ain't fuckin' this boy. No sir."

"Jesus Christ, Fillmore," Stace replied, "he ain't come down from heaven, y'know."

"I don't want him hurt."

"You done said that."

"And I meant it."

Fillmore delivered those words before moving his marvelous mouth between my buttocks. There he too placed that outlaw, that renegade of kisses, deeper, more shuddering in its implication than any other could ever be. And taken to its last, pungent frontier, it was made even more wondrous in meaning with the penetration of that tight ring by a furled tongue. I felt then, right then, being slowly turned in Fillmore's artful manipulations, that if with my whole body I could create the same pleasure of utter abandon that was being created by his mouth and tongue in my butthole then I would be forever happy on my back, legs at a hoist while someone did something, well, anything, to me there. But then, not everyone could have encountered the technique that I had on that first foray, for not only did Fillmore kiss, lick, lap, suck, prod, and rim that favored dropchute, he also blew on it in a steady, cool stream, a zephyr wind gentle upon the curlicue. I felt then, and I feel now, privileged that these transitions were initiated in the company of those men and not in some boiler room or rectory with a terse denizen lacking even a rudimentary concern for, or an understanding of, a boy bursting from the hot, pregnant bulb of expectation into full sexual flower.

"Man oh man, Fillmore," Stace said. "Maybe I can't fuck that asshole but it's sure some hot suckin' you're doin' on it."

With one hand at the back of Fillmore's neck Stace started to jack off with deep deliberate strokes.

"Yeah, baby, suck that kid's shit chute." He slapped at Fillmore with his dick. "Eat his asshole."

And so Stace, the big man, the hard man, the man urged yet again to fuck, moved behind Fillmore, his form looming over he who loomed over me. Pausing and then, like an cache of slipping stones long overdue for a plunge, he tumbled onto Fillmore's back, shoving his cock, impatient and imperious, up the ass, oh God, brutally up the ass, of the man I then loved. The acceptance quick and the accommodation quicker, Fillmore and Stace began a tug between them that was seamless and devoid of flaw, the cock and anus well-fitted, well-tempered, evenly acquainted to the ditch right then being plowed.

I was entering from the trap door into the kingdom of sodomy.

Bigger than all the life I had ever known, the sheer size, complexity, and meaning of the effort in the mounting being done above excited me in ways I had no idea existed, could not measure, and were far beyond my logical comprehension. But what I did know, without words, was that I was afire with more intensity, with more desire wanting more release delivered from a higher plane than, I was sure, could ever be served on this planet. I was awash in passion, a tender victim, come new to feed on and—God, it was true—to be fed to love. In that churning moment of that churning confusion with Fillmore seeking to gain from me an explosion that I would give only too willingly, I worked in the syncopation of our encounter, our effort knowing our very libidos would soon collide in manly triumph. Stace was in a grand parade of monumental fucking, surging pell-mell toward its only conclusion amid popping muscles and running sweat. I had been taken to the edge with Fillmore's grip on my balls and his tongue moving over the head of my peter and curling about the slit. Then he plunged down on the shaft, time after time and yet time again, coaxing me, bullying me, pushing me until the precarious balance was lost, oh boy, so very gratefully lost, and the plague was thrown off, the conquest ended, the exquisitely sickening exhilaration of the triumph beginning, and the *real* ejaculation— in the presence of real men, really handsome, queer men—was now at last a fact. In attendance were all the dancers, jugglers and magicians necessary to fulfill all the gaudy promises as I erupted into Fillmore's waiting mouth, his very still mouth. I soared in songs that I wanted to sing out at the top of my lungs—holler!—as the event unfolded as it should, and always would.

God!

And then shrinking into a passive dwindle, smaller and smaller spasms chased those larger until there were no more; all melted, gone, lost. I felt the craziest aloneness ever. Everything was different—so different—and still the same.

Yet a neophyte in an expedition of this type, my own gremlins now enervated and tied down, I was, in the inexperience of youth and thus spent, ready to end the game. I was therefore a little disturbed by the tumult still being conducted above me. Among adults such grapplings outside myth and magic were fearful and threatening. The two virile men still engaged in a mutually agreed upon struggle were indeed intimidating to watch. Being images of the future, clear and gritty, and, of course, exciting too, they were far removed from the drench of the rosy—and probably in some respects prissy—passion I was then entertaining. Stace, his fantastic cock moving him toward the gate, was sweating in torrents, his lips curled in a self-absorbed sneer. Mounted as he was on the slender and elegant Fillmore, whose face mirrored the hearty tribulation that marked the spin they were embarked upon, Stace embodied in my young eyes the raptorial bent of some men in these affairs. Being young and straight of vision then, the curve of history has since shown the fact to be not nearly so harsh. The man was, in the glittering light of retrospection, heroic and audacious.

"Fillmore!" he shouted. "You made that little shit come."

"Yeah!"

"You sucked his peter and then his sweet little puddin' hole, and you made him come."

"Yeah!"

Fillmore heaved his butt back at Stace, the strain in the effort distending his beauty.

"Yeah! And he came in my mouth, Stace," he said. "The kid shot his fuckin' wad in my mouth."

"In your fuckin' mouth, bitch."

"It was like sweet, sticky honey."

"Like fuckin' honey, bitch."

They were up now, two beings of an unknown forest, upright and involved in their tangle, the parts of it just beginning with the penis/anus union. Stace gripped Fillmore's genitals, cock and balls, the package, as if to claim them for his own. The cock stood out, straight out and hard, magnificent as it gathered to deliver.

"And now, you horny humper," Stace bellowed, "you got my cock up *your* fuckin' meat hole."

"Yeah! Up my fuckin' asshole."

They were sweating and at an awful strain.

"Fuck you, Fillmore."

"Fuck me, Stace. Yeah, big fella, fuck me."

Then, leaning forward, Fillmore opened himself to Stace as fully as ever could be possible. Taking a wide, flatfooted stance and bending forward and pulling his buttocks apart with his hands, he assumed a simian posture in essence so primitive, so laden with utter compliance that Stace pulled the man off his feet. Off his feet! And the fuck continued with Fillmore riding on Stace's haunches, the strokes now jabs, tight, closed jabs with the weapon lost deep within.

"I'm comin', Fillmore!" Stace shouted, his huge voice filling the cave with echoes. "I'm comin', Fillmore!"

"Shoot the works, Stace."

"In your fuckin' butthole."

"In my fuckin' butthole."

"Butthole!"

"My fuckin' butthole."

They shook and trembled with the effort.

When Stace started his pumping, Fillmore regained his flatfooted position and remained still as his partner played out his moment, there coming with the semen the twists, the shudders, the sighs, the grunts of the delicious torture until, the abatement almost complete, Fillmore worked his cock in a fast jackoff while making spiraling movements upon Stace's still embedded prick. In his jerking drive toward orgasm, Fillmore brought the shot right up to the brink. And then—and by God he was magnificent—Fillmore, in a most unsimian-like manner, pulled away from Stace and turned, and the big man fell to his knees, his mouth open to receive the cock and acquire its spurtings, hot, thick, and sticky.

"You got that cum, butthole fucker?" Fillmore demanded.

Stace nodded, his mouth full of cock and jizz'm, his hands empty in the dust at Fillmore's feet.

Fillmore pulled his cock from Stace's mouth, letting it slide across the side of his face. "Now swallow that cum, butthole fucker."

Stace swallowed and then looked up at Fillmore who's face shone with a wide smile, the brilliant smile of indulgence.

"By God Almighty's cunt," he said, "that was great." He took a grip on Fillmore's arm and pulled himself erect.

I watched as the two men recovered and reassembled their unobtrusive, country butch identities, brushing bits of debris from one another, jabbing and fondling, laughing. I began to feel—and not by any means the first time, either—the emptiness of imminent abandonment.

I got to my knees, trying to find my shorts.

My butt was toward Stace.

"Hey, kid," he boomed.

I turned.

He was working his mighty hips into his jeans.

"If you're lucky, kiddo," he said, "maybe Fillmore'll show you how a real man takes a fuckin' up the ass. And then someday it might be you who gets lucky. Who knows?"

Fillmore looked at me, his good looks alone enough to make me want to bawl. He winked and smiled, nodding his head toward Stace.

"He's okay, Duane," he said. "There ain't nothin' to worry about."

"No," Stace said, "not for now."

"Now, shit, Stace... "

"I said not for now, didn't I?"

They laughed, Stace and Fillmore. They seemed to be able to communicate with something other than words.

"Say, you know what?" Stace said. "I'd sure like to see Wobble and this boy get together. That's sure be a slick picture. Man!"

I looked at Fillmore. He was dressed now and looking as cool and perfect and collected as a bible student. I finished pulling on my shorts and hurried into my jeans.

"They're probably about the same age," Fillmore said.

"And about the same size too," Stace replied. "Though Wobble's really startin' to get his growth now."

Fillmore laughed. "That's about as far as any similarities go. There ain't no kid I ever seen that's faster'n Wobble. In anything."

"To be sure," Stace agreed. And then after a pause, he said, "So whattaya think, Fillmore?"

Fillmore put his hand on my shoulder. "We can introduce 'em, I guess, and see what happens."

"I know what'll happen," Stace said.

I looked up at Fillmore. "Who's Wobble?"

"Oh," Fillmore said, "Wobble's a kid that emigrated over here from someplace like Poland or Belgium, and... "

Stace interrupted, "His name can't be said in American, so we call him Wobble."

"... and," Fillmore continued, "he works on his uncle's place about a half a mile or so over the cane scrub. The boy don't talk hardly none at all. He's nice enough. He just don't talk much."

"But, by God, he sure knows about fuckin' and suckin'," Stace said.

Stace came and stood by Fillmore. After a moment he put his hand on my shoulder and squeezed.

I felt included.

And I felt good.

I felt warm.

"Don't go gettin' big ideas, Stace," Fillmore said. "I said we'd arrange a meetin' sometime. That's all. If the boys hit it off all right, maybe then we'll see about doin' any other stuff."

"I do swear, Fillmore," Stace said, "sometimes I think you should teach Sunday school. You seem to know all about how things are right and wrong and all that."

Fillmore shook his head like he was annoyed.

"And," Stace added, "I *know* sure as hell you're pretty enough."

Stace put his hand at the back of Fillmore's neck and, pulling his head forward, planted a long kiss on his lips.

Standing close to these men, being near them in all this wonder as it unfolded before me almost as if in a dream, I had a fleeting impression of the future, hazy and indistinct as if induced by fever, where for as long as time lasted there would be we three, Stace, Fillmore, and me, aligned in this marvelous configuration of impossible perfection.

"C'mon, you guys," Stace said, "let's go."

After we'd followed the trail out from beneath the bridge and were walking along the road toward the hog barns and yards Fillmore started to sing in a beautiful, mellow tenor. Soon Stace joined in with a less than show-stopping baritone. But that wasn't important. It was more than enough that they felt free to sing at all. They sang easy songs, silly songs, and often, just parts of songs. Frequently they'd touch one another, on the shoulder, the chest, an arm, on the side of the face.

Often they'd touch me too as I walked between them.

At the gate to the lane leading up to the hog parlor Stace stopped and leaned against the white rail fence.

"Y'know," he said, "day after tomorrow Mr. Dickens is goin' up Colton to see the doctor. He'll be gone almost all day. Why don't we just mosey on over and see how Wobble's doin'?"

I could see from the look on Fillmore's face that he didn't think that was too good an idea. Mr. Dickens, the foreman, was pretty strict in his expectations of what he wanted done as far as work was concerned.

"I don't know, Stace," Fillmore said.

"That'll be Tuesday," Stace said. "I can do on Monday most of what we're gonna be doin' on Tuesday. Nothin' to it."

"We'll see," Fillmore said.

"That's good enough, sweetheart," Stace said grinning. "I just love to hear you say 'we'll see'."

Well, come Tuesday at about noon we were following the ruts of a narrow road along a dry ditch through the cane scrub. Squatty clumps of willow grew among the cane, and the dirt was dry, hard, and black. Circling a fallen down shack, the road went low into a hollow and then up a short rise. Turning sharp it went on another hundred yards or so, made another sharp turn, and then passed through a laurel hedge into a pasture of the greenest, deepest damned grass I've ever seen. Cows—and even I could tell they weren't ordinary cows—grazed on that perfect grass. They moved slowly about their pleasure as if in regal disposition.

That farm seemed the perfect farm, perfect where every detail from the shaping of the arches of rose bushes to the red hinges on the wooden gates seemed looked after with finicky concern. We went down a lane lined with small, round trees. The spaces between were spread with pink gravel smoothly raked. At the end of the lane was a barn with green shutters and yellow trim. There was a tower with weather vane on the roof. Everything was as pretty as a picture.

"Hey, Wobble," Stace called as we went into the barn. "Are you in here, boy? It's us, Stace and Fillmore, and we come over to see how you might be doin' these days."

There were sounds of activity from shadows in the back, under a pitched roof.

"Is that you, Wobble?" Stace called.

"I over here."

"He's in the corn crib," Fillmore said.

We went between a pair of posts, about three feet apart, and stood at the end of a long bin filled with corn. Dry and hard and golden and gray, red and black, it looked like the hoarded wealth of an acquisitive noble with ambitious but simple tastes, and standing there in the piles of that wealth was a boy. Stripped to the waist, his skin was light; he glowed almost white in the dim light, like a dream of a fine possession. His jeans, baggy and loose, were gathered around his middle with a wide leather belt. His chest, while boyishly thin, was wider and more muscular than mine, and his arms were slender and well-formed with muscles pushing toward development. Wearing large gray gloves with blue backs, he pitched a bushel basket of corn over his shoulder and then fell to his knees.

"Hi there, Wobble," Stace greeted.

And Fillmore said, "How're ya doin', fella."

Wobble peered out at us through the slats of the corn crib. His eyes, astonishingly blue in a sort of abstract vacuity, moved slowly from Stace to Fillmore and then to me, and then back to Stace again. His face was wide, his cheek bones high, his mouth full, his nose flat.

"This here's Duane," Stace said.

Wobble looked at me quickly and then at Fillmore once again.

"American boy?" he said softly.

"Sure enough," Stace said. "And an American *city* boy to boot."

Wobble vaulted over the side of the crib as if stepping across a threshold and, pulling off his glove, offered me his hand.

His grip was manly and hard; our handshake was stiff and brief.

"You American boy," he said, smiling shyly. "You American boy by God holy shit."

"From Tulsa," Stace said.

"Tulsa, Oklahoma," I clarified.

"Yeah. Tulsa, Oklahoma," Stace repeated very clearly to Wobble. "Yeah. That's a big, big American city we got."

And then to me he said, "He likes things about American cities. Most foreigners like him do because I guess they didn't get to have much nice stuff over there in the old lands of Poland and Belgium and the like."

I turned and smiled at Wobble.

With lightening speed he did maybe three or four handsprings backward and then sprung upward to grab hold of a two-by-four over the corn crib. Another deft movement put him in a disarmingly casual perch above us.

"I guess he's happy to meet you, Duane," Fillmore said.

"Shit, that boy's more'n just happy," Stace said. "Why, I'd say he's fuckin' joyful."

"I fuckin' joyful," Wobble crowed from his perch and then flew from it in a somersault to land on his feet just inches in front of Stace and Fillmore.

"Wobble fuckin' joyful," he cried, his chest out, his shoulders back, his face a mirror of youthful enthusiasm.

He looked at Stace.

"Fuckin'-a, you cute little fuck bucket," Stace said. "And you got good fuckin' reason to be. You're gonna be an American boy too."

"Wobble fuckin'-a American boy too holy shit."

I looked at Fillmore.

"He talks okay," I said.

Stace laughed.

"Shit yes, he talks okay," he said. "He'll talk a streak if he hears you say it first."

"Actually I'd say," Fillmore replied, "that he cusses a whole lot more than he talks."

Wobble grinned.

Stace walked to a six-by-six post and smacked it a couple of times with the palm of his hand. Hard.

"Well, Fillmore," he said, "what say you and me take a walk over to the ice house and see if anybody's there. Let's, like you said, let the boys get acquainted."

Fillmore looked at me and then at Wobble and then, after a pause, nodded and said, "Okay."

"Where's the ice house?" I asked.

"Wobble knows," Stace said. "Don't ya, Wobble?"

Wobble was vigorous in nodding his head.

Then Stace and Fillmore, Stace throwing an arm across Fillmore's shoulders, left the barn.

I looked at Wobble.

Now that the men were gone and they apparently having been a large source of his bravado, he seemed to retreat into shyness. Not being overly adept at engineering social intercourse myself, I cast about for some way to establish a connection.

"Show me how you do the flips again," I said.

"Flips?"

"Yeah, the flips."

I made a turning gesture with my hand.

"Oh," he said nodding. "That's flips?"

"Unhuh."

"I do flips. You fuckin'-a bet, American boy."

Wobble unfastened his wide belt, and the loose, ill-fitting jeans fell to his ankles. He kicked them aside. Beneath he wore a black brief that was tight over the small hard globes of his butt and around his thighs. Now his torso was in perfect proportion with the rest of his body, tall and slender and white, and held with assurance and poise.

"Now Wobble do fuckin' good flips," he said.

With astonishing speed he did three backward flips, balanced on his hands for several seconds with his legs pressed together and straight, and then bounded back forward, higher and wider this time. That was followed by a series of cartwheels, slow and graceful and elegant, that ended in a couple of neat pirouettes. Then he executed a whole string of fast handsprings, going this way and that, until, in one high vault, he sailed up and grabbed the two-by-four, made a turn and hoisted himself up, fell back, and then hung there, by his knees, looking down at me.

Oh God, he was a beautiful creature, and, seeking approval, his grin was enchantingly direct. Gazing on his body hanging there long, lean, and lithe and his chest in a healthy heave, I felt in my own being a surge of energy, and with it an immediate need to grab hold and hold on and be hauled up and through all manner of wonderful impossibility.

I felt courted.

I felt demure.

I felt perfect.

And then moving upright, Wobble, as he'd done before, propelled himself from the two-by-four in a high leap and landed, with a thump, on his feet squarely before me.

"Oh Jesus," I murmured. "Oh Jesus, Wobble, that was wonderful."

"American boy like?"

"Oh yes."

He put his hands on my hip, and then moved and patted my butt.

"American boy fuckin' handsome little shit."

I looked down. The thin mesh of Wobble's brief showed through with the bulbous fullness of his cock and balls. One bulb strained much fuller that the others.

"Ho ho," Wobble laughed, "American boy neat-o kid. He like cock."

He grabbed my hand and put it on the bulb protruding toward me within the black mesh.

"Okay, American boy? We fuckin' play sex game?"

I nodded.

Pulling, but hardly, Wobble led me toward the corn crib. We climbed through the narrow opening and stood inside. The heaps of ears shone with that ancient and durable richness.

Wobble stripped off his briefs.

"American boy get naked too," he said.

Wobble's cock stood straight out at a stiff strain. The alabastrine head pushed through a foreskin that draped across the opening with casual elegance. He put his hand under his scrotum, raising it up and thrusting the whole package, cock and balls, toward me.

I hesitated, but not meaning to.

"Please American boy get naked too," Wobble said, his green eyes liquid with supplication.

I stripped off my clothes, bending away to put them in a pile. Wobble ran his hand over my back, across my butt.

"American boy got fuckin' number one nice assbutt," he said holding his cock tightly, like a weapon. "Assbutt number one fuckin' hot place for Wobble meat. Bend over, American boy."

Unable to do anything but, I bent over.

"Oh pretty, pretty, poppy," Wobble crooned while dancing his fingers on my asshole. "Oh, pretty, pretty, poppy flower in cute American boy assbutt."

I felt the warm, smooth flesh of Wobble's cock replace his fingers, his fingers moving to a grip on my cock.

"Is American boy fuckin' hot for Wobble cock up pretty assbutt poppy flower?" he said.

"Oh yes. Oh yes."

"Yes?"

"Yes."

The spit Wobble gathered was warm and slick as he prepared me between my buttocks, his fingers working around the hole. Then one went in. The pain was a thin, familiar stranger. I waited while Wobble finger fucked me, pushing and turning and crooking. Then taking my cock in a hard grip he began the old jackoff caper and when the smooth persuasion had begun its swing, he pulled his finger from my asshole. His stiff cock then between us, he leaned into me, pressed into me, and, with the low glide of a goose into a sluice, he made his entrance up my butt. The thick probe brought a pain of warmth, of fulfilled purpose, and in the following repetitions of urgent pulse we were wrapped, push by push, in the wet cocoon of sodomy. Wobble's hands were on my hips, my back, then my shoulders and neck. They went down my arms and to my chest.

"American boy good fuck for hot fuckin' Wobble meat."

I swung my ass and dipped my knees, rolling with the thrill of the thick dick being forced into me time after time.

"American boy like Wobble fuck?"

"Yes."

"American boy like hot Wobble fuck up assbutt?"

"Yes."

The pace of the penetration quickened, the depth sought grew deeper. Bent forward with my hands on my knees, my ass the focus of one lust spinning within another, I felt draped in lavish robes and hung with tinkling baubles, and all of the tackiest, cheapest, gaudiest grandeur possible. I was rolling into the station of cornhole heaven.

"Ho ho! Ho ho!" Wobble shouted, "American boy gonna get Wobble jizz up assbutt!"

"Yes!"

"American boy gonna get Wobble jizz up assbutt! Gonna get Wobble jizz up assbutt... Wobble jizz up... jizz up assbutt... jizz up... jizz up... "

With the muscular banging of Wobble's hips against my butt I felt the fierce churning of cock in my asshole. In the ram and jam, I felt the determined drive toward the promised eruption, toward the ultimate spew, toward the... well, yes.

And in seconds it arrived.

Wobble's frame stiffened against mine, his hands gripped my shoulders, and with a stream of garbled words he delivered his shipment of steamy jizz up my ass.

Bent over I waited, my cock hard in my hand and at a seep with its own load of sap.

In a moment, Wobble pulled out of my asshole and popped me smartly on the butt. The withdrawal was shocking in its finality.

"Stand up, American boy."

Standing, I turned, the head of my cock a glossy mottled pink.

"Good," Wobble muttered. "Now Wobble get hot jizz in mouth."

Going to his knees with his mouth wide open and putting his hands on my hips, Wobble devoured my cock in one enthusiastic and complete gobble. With my asshole still burning from the stretch of its recent fucking and my nuts throbbing in search of release, that rapid engulfment induced the sharp jabbing threats of ejaculation in my penis ready to do their wicked dance. Going for broke I thrust my hips at Wobble's face. Taking the attack with ease and maintaining the penetration long enough for a few shudders and jerks to run my body, he backed off to the head and delivered there maddeningly slow and perfectly precise caresses with his lips and tongue. While I whirled in the thrill of those delights, his hands grasped my buttocks and squeezed, a few of his squeezing fingers tickling my asshole adding to the sweet injury done my asshole even sweeter insults. I quivered and quaked, staggered and wheeled, and, in a tight twisting of the greed in my soul, I sent out and into Wobble's mouth thick spurts of all the hope and despair that dwell in life's hotter, darker places.

Wobble took the stuff like a trouper. And then gentle in the licking, he nursed the organ through its wilt and shrink, and back into its passive wait of soft anticipation.

Leaning back he looked up. "American boy shoot big fuckin' load!"

Sapped and sopping with a wealth of wet, goofy feelings, I grinned like an idiot confronted with idiocy.

89

Wobble leapt up.

"We fuckin' go ice house now," he said.

The ice house, whatever its history, wasn't the big red brick building I was expecting, not like the one at Fifteenth and Main in Tulsa. This sorry place was—when we got to it off in a thicket of willow scrub and berry vines along a stagnant creek—a pile of granite stones under a leaning roof of collapsing timbers. Backwaters murkily purple and green harbored the creatures of whirr, buzz, and croak. Bird calls were thin and plaintive.

Trailing Wobble up a ramp and around a heavy plank door fallen free of its hinges we went into a cool, dark maze of weathered wood, mossy stonework, and rusted pipes hanging from beams and posts. Rank vines with large green leaves clambered about in heavy dominance. The litter common to places of extended and forgotten decline lay about.

"No here," Wobble said.

"Who? Stace and Fillmore?"

Wobble shrugged.

"Nobody no here," he said.

Looking around and then nodding his head, Wobble motioned for me to follow.

Not far away along a catwalk of creaking boards the hulk of an old boat lay low in the green water, its bow pushed into the muddy bank. The cabin was covered with a tattered blue plastic tarp, the edges frayed and knotted like the lazy lace of the demented.

Wobble held a finger to his lips and cocked his head, listening.

There were muffled sounds of activity inside.

Wobble motioned and we crept quietly aboard and crouched down behind some broken crates.

"Now come on, you all,"—it was a voice from inside, high and sort of nasal—"I don't have a whole lot of time."

"Just hold your stitches there, Malcolm, and take off your damned pants because"—this I recognized as Stace's voice—"no matter what kinda hurry you're in, this takes a little time if it's gonna be done nice like it should be. Ain't that right, Fillmore?"

"That's right, Stace."

"Well of *course* I want it to be as nice as it can be, but I *still* don't have a lot of time."

"You already made that known, Malcolm," Stace said. "We don't want to see those fine, pressed trousers mussed, do we?"

"No, they're Italian silk."

"So you better take 'em off and lay 'em to the side."

"Yes, I guess you're right."

A pause.

"Say, Malcolm, it looks like you went and got yourself a cute little tattoo since we last seen you."

"And on your pretty butt too."

"*That* was Jeff's idea."

"Very becoming, don't you think, Fillmore?"

"Very much so."

"Never mind the damned tattoo, let's just get on... "

"Right."

Wobble shook his head.

"I no understand," he whispered.

I shrugged my shoulders. What could *I* say?

Wobble inched his way up to the cabin and found a rip in the tarp. Pulling it down slightly, he uncovered a small round window.

He peered in while I listened.

"Oh heavens, Stace,"—it was the Malcolm voice again—"it's obvious you haven't shrunk in size. Oh my heavens no. Oh dear, let me throw a suck or two on that."

_ I heard Stace laugh. "Okay, but turn a bit thataway so's Fillmore can get at your butt."

There was a thump and a pause.

"Oh God, this place is such a dump."

"Shit, Malcolm, it ain't a cotillion we're tryin' to conduct here. Just turn your butt to Fillmore."

"I will if you move that damned box."

"Okay."

"That's good," Fillmore said. "Now spread your feet, Malcolm."

"Like that?"

"Yeah, and squat down some. Not too much."

"Like that"

"Yeah, that's good. That's good," Fillmore said.

"Yeah, real good," Stace agreed. "Now suck away, Malcolm."

"While it's the fuckin' I tend to," Fillmore said.

"Get a nice wide spread between those butt cheeks, Fillmore," Stace said. "I like to watch you push that stiff meat up somebody's asshole... "

"I'm a Godhigh, Stace," the Malcolm voice said. "I'm Malcolm Winslow Godhigh the Third. I'm not just *somebody*."

"Christ, I know who you are, Malcolm. I'm only talkin', you know. I'm only playin' the game."

"Malcolm," Fillmore said, "just suck."

"Well, I don't like... "

"Just suck, Malcolm."

"Okay."

Wobble was deeply engrossed in what he was seeing through the window. He kept moving his head this way and that as if to improve his view. His hand was on his crotch massaging and I could see a swelling bulge there. Even if for the moment it seemed I'd been left out, I was still intrigued by the varied capabilities of this young fellow from the old country. While watching him I listened to the voices, my own interest more than strongly lascivious.

"Oh, oh, ohhhh, Fillmore. You haven't lost anything either. Oh dear. Oh dear! Jesus Christ!"

A pause.

"Oh God. Oh Jesus," the Malcolm voice said in a soft supplication, "that feels soooo nice."

"You're lookin' good, buddy-boy," Stace said. "You got that big ole knob in there okay. Now give 'im the shaft. Ha ha!"

"Bad joke, Stace."

"Do tell," Stace replied. "So how ya doin', Malcolm? Just nod your noggin a little if you're havin' a good time."

"That looked like a nod to me," Fillmore said.

"Oh hell yes. Malcolm is always up for havin' a good time. He's a good cocksucker too. Gives some of the best head in the county."

"He's got a smooth sweet butthole in a smooth sweet ass too. He's got to be one of the best butthole fucks around."

"You got that right, Fillmore. Yep, you got that right. He's one excellent cocksucker and one prime pieces of ass."

"Yes sir."

"Okay, you guys," the Malcolm voice said, "you can lay off the country bumpkin flattery. I didn't just get on this train, you know. I'm here to suck some cock and get fucked."

"And we're the guys who can do it."

"So let's do it."

"Of this particular moment," Fillmore said, "you seem the one that's responsible for doin' the cock suckin' around here."

"Okay. I'll suck and you fuck."

"I got it. You got it, Stace?"

"Oh I'm gonna get it, Fillmore."

Wobble had worked his jeans open and his dick out. The thing seemed even bigger, brighter, and more serious looking than before. He was running his hand on it in the coaxing rub ancient of the centuries, running his hand up the shaft to the head and then, after pausing there for a squeeze, slipping back to the root in the delicate fleece of golden hair.

"Fillmore!" Stace called, "how's it goin', buddy-boy?"

"Goin' hot hell for leather, Stace."

"Got good ass, there?"

"Real good ass. You got good suckin' there?"

"Mighty good suckin'. Some of the best ever."

A pause.

"Oh shit!"

"Oh man, looks like you're about to blow your nuts, Fillmore."

Another pause.

"Yeah, Stace, this load is damn near a goner."

Wobble looked at me, his face a wash of insipid foolishness, his smile a fatuous simper. Summoning me with a jerk of his head, I went on all fours, sidling like a sideshow clown, and took his cock, the obvious proposition, into my mouth. He sighed and I started sucking, the sucking here an extension of all the sucking anywhere, of anyone, by anyone.

"Oh Stace! Oh Malcolm! Oh God, I'm gonna fuckin' blow!"

"Fuckin' blow, buddy-boy. Blow that fuckin' load!"

"Get ready, Malcolm... "

"I'm ready, Fillmore."

A pause of heavy breathing, grunts of exertion.

93

"Grab hold of your balls, you guys," Fillmore muttered. "Here comes a hot load of grease."

A pause of intense quiet, of dangling expectation.

"Now! Fuckin' now!"

Fillmore's voice, voice of calmness and moderation, was raised up in timbre to the pitch of the masculine hysteria, the twisted frenzy that is bound into the gift granted us in the kissing of God's asshole.

"Fuckin' hallelujah!" Fillmore shouted. "Hallefuckin'lujah!

"Go, Fillmore!"

A pause of patient indulgence, and then...

"And now, fellas," Stace announced, "I'm gonna get into that hole myself—I so dearly do *love* sloppy seconds—and get me a nice piece of Malcolm's butt pie."

"Please do," the Malcolm voice said.

Then Fillmore said, "That's a fine lookin' boner you're workin' on there, Malcolm."

"Oh my, isn't it now," the Malcolm voice agreed. "And the handsome nuts you seeing hanging below are hot with a load of thick jizz waiting for somebody's mouth."

"So hey, Fillmore," Stace said, "why don'tcha get down and swing on Malcolm's dong while I put the prod to his bung."

"I'd call that deal," Fillmore replied.

"Oh you bet, baby," the Malcolm voice added.

Wobble's dick was pulsing in my mouth as I worked it with the suck born of my soul, and while I sucked I kept the beat on my own stiff meat with my fist. And then Wobble touched me on the head, and when I looked up, the knob of his cock in my mouth, he smiled with the benevolence of a monk. But, oh dear, hot behind that beaming sweetness came a dispatch of cum-snot terrific in velocity. Immediately my mouth was filled with jizz cream, rich with its taint of stigma. Shocked—and pleased—I swallowed, and in the swallowing I was smacked with a feeling of utter and liberating depravity, the utter part being the impeccable simplicity of it all, the liberating part being the clear—and believe me it *was* perfectly clear, my dear—implication carried in relishing the creep and slide of jizz clots down my throat, and the depravity part... well, I guess that's pretty obvious.

"Oh fuck!" the Malcolm voice exclaimed. "Oh fuck the gods of

Olympus! Fuck those handsome beauties. And fuck me, Stace! Fuck me, fuck me, fuck me. Oh! Oh! Oh! Oh fuck me hard, Stace! Oh! Oh! Oh! Oh fuck, I'm going to come! I'm going to... I'm coming! Take it, Fillmore!"

"Atta boy, Malcolm!" Stace yelled. "Shoot that good jizz into Fillmore's mouth. Pop that shit down the dude's throat!"

"Oh dear! Oh fucking dear!"

A pause of desperate elation.

"And, Malcolm my baby doll, here we go again!" Stace shouted. "Oh yeah, here comes one neat slug of nut juice for you too!"

"Shoot, Stace!"

Stace's voice sang out high and wide and with a mile of expletives, glorious and direct and hung with all the glitter and drip of the entire game of homosexual fuck.

And then there was silence, a curiously expectant silence, perhaps of a sort that might follow a really grisly murder. Not even the birds or bugs made a sound.

I lay with my head in Wobble's lap, his cock still in my mouth, the lovely thing long ago returned to its patient wait. I was floating in the euphoria of the immediate past, a past so transient as to deny definition, and yet somehow I was aware of the burdens being assembled for me for a lengthy and sometimes more than likely trying journey. I wondered idly, my tongue making a wet wrapping of itself around Wobble's penis, how long Wobble—or someone like him—might be with me in the trek.

"Ho ho there, boys!"

Stace stood in the cabin door, his mammoth body dwarfing the tiny structure. "I had me a hunch we was bein' treated the privilege of a bit of eavesdroppin'."

I put my sex stuff away with due haste, but Wobble did his collecting with the silken self-possession of a cat.

Fillmore came out and, standing and grinning with Stace, said, "I'll be damned if it ain't Wobble and Duane. What do you make of that, Stace!"

"Who is it out there?" came the Malcolm voice.

"It's Wobble and Duane."

"You mean that foreign kid and... and who else did you say?"

"Duane. The boy come over here from Tulsa."

"Do I know him?"

95

"I don't think so."

"Are you sure?"

"Yeah."

"The name sounds familiar."

We were then joined by an elegantly slender fellow, a blondly handsome product of sustained good breeding, and who with limpid blue eyes gave me a fast once-over.

After a moment he said, "The way we're all *standing* here you'd think we were waiting on someone important."

"Nope, nobody important comin' here," Stace said. "Not to no sunk boat in a swamp."

"This is Malcolm, Duane," Fillmore said. "And this is Duane, Malcolm."

Malcolm seemed to take my offered hand as if it wasn't the best idea he ever had.

"That big white house you see on the hill above the pecan orchards is where Malcolm lives," Fillmore said.

"Pecan orchards planted years and years ago," Stace added. "Yessir, trees planted years and years ago by Malcolm's old granddaddy, a fine Southern gentleman who's now dead in the dust."

Casting Stace a thin stare Malcolm said to me, "Are you acquainted with the Tulsa VanDamms, Duane?"

"No."

"The Blankenships?"

"No."

"Well, do you have family there?"

"What I have is there I guess."

"I see."

Malcolm turned on his heel.

"I've simply *got* to run along," he said patting and smoothing and arranging himself. "I'd love to stay and continue in this marvelous little chat but I simply *must* go."

"So how's about givin' us a lift, Malcolm?" Stace said.

"I'm driving the Mercedes. It's a coupe, you know, and I... "

"Yeah," Fillmore said. "We got us more bodies here than your car's got room for."

"We could pile in," Stace said, grinning. "It ain't far we're goin'. Shit, that'd be fun!"

Malcolm looked suddenly stricken.

"You do understand, don't you, my dear?" he said. "About the car?"

"Oh sure, my dear," Stace said. "Understandin' ain't hard at all."

And so Malcolm, lovely and flowing in silk and substance, made away along the planks, his fine patent leather shoes treading dangerously close to the muddy, murky water.

"The dude comes to fuck us and suck us but he can't give us a ride," Stace muttered.

"Well, you wasn't *your* sweetest of selfs neither," Fillmore said.

Stace laughed. "I never am with Malcolm. I make it a point."

"It ain't his fault he was raised up with airs," Fillmore said.

"Why honey, Malcolm'd have airs if he'd been raised up with hogs," Stace said. "Now c'mon, let's forget about Malcolm. He gets some of what he wants from us, and we get some of what we want from him. Nothin' could be simpler." He paused, a slight frown crossing his blandly handsome face. "But, lookie here, we got us two little fellas who like us— for the time bein' anyway—just the way we are."

Stace put one huge hand on Wobble's shoulder and the other on mine and laughed. "Well now, young fellas, how you all been gettin' along, huh? You been gettin' some things straight between you? Haha!"

I nodded, and glancing at Wobble I felt surge of flush warm my face.

Wobble grinned.

"Why lookie there, Fillmore!" Stace exclaimed. "Duane's blushin' and Wobble looks like he swallowed a canary. Yessir, these boys are gonna be pals sure enough."

Wobble set his legs in a manly stance and pushed back his shoulders, his wide face a gleam of satisfaction.

"American boy is fuckin-a hot stuff!" he yelled, his voice a trumpet of conviction.

"It's Duane. His name is Duane," Fillmore said looking directly at Wobble. "Doo-ane. Say it, Wobble. Say, Doo-ane."

Wobble looked at Stace, quickly at me, and then back at Fillmore.

"Doo-ane," Fillmore repeated.

"Doo... Doo-ane," Wobble said softly. "Doo-ane."

97

"That's right, Wobble," Fillmore said. "That's perfect."

"Doo-ane," Wobble said looking at me.

I smiled the best I could in trying to hide the fact that I felt like a dope, and also that I felt very good.

"By God, I'm hungry!" boomed Stace. "I'm hungry enough to eat the girdle off a pregnant snake. If we can get somebody to give us a ride into town I'll buy us the biggest and best pizza they got at Hannibal's."

"Let's go," Fillmore said. "It ain't often we get to hear that."

And so we left that boat sunk—and probably destined to stay sunk forever—in a swamp and went along the catwalk to the ice house, and then out through the thicket to the road.

We trudged along for a while, and in that trudge—Stace and Fillmore gone ahead a few paces—I soon felt the light press of Wobble's arm across my shoulders.

I turned and looked up into his face.

"I fuckin'-a like cute American boy Doo-ane," he said.

I smiled feeling a curious sort of expectation flow about me.

"And," Wobble said, his voice going to a whisper, "I sure gonna fuckin'-a fuck cute American boy Doo-ane too. Lots."

I felt a tingle of thrill join that expectation.

Pretty soon a truck loaded with crates full of chickens stopped. We all found places to sit and, laughing and talking, went off to town for the promised pizza.

Well, it was then just early May that summer in Arkansas.

I wasn't due back in Oklahoma until the first week of September.

At the earliest.

Jesus Christ!

THREE

BRIDGES

Matt had this sort of romance goin' with bridges.

He knew about all of them—well, the big ones anyway—all around the world. There was pictures of bridges put up on all the walls of the shack he and his grandpa lived in out on rural route 18 just a quarter mile or so past the We Kill 'Em—U-Pluck 'Em chicken ranch.

On the first day I met him and he'd guided the conversation around to bridges, Matt said to me, "In the whole world my favorites are only maybe three hundred miles from here. They're the Golden Gate Bridge and the San Francisco-Oakland Bay Bridge out there in California."

"California, eh?" I said.

"That's right."

"Do you like California?"

"Well, I don't really know nothin' much about California. What I'm talkin' about here is them wonderful bridges they got out there."

"Oh, I see."

Well, I fell in love with the little fella—he was just under five-four and cute as a box of brown buttons—after I sucked him off maybe a week or so later on a Friday mornin' while were sittin' out front in my beat-up pickup waitin' on the mailman. Some crows was makin' a hell of a racket in a dead tree across the road, and the white, flat Nevada sky looked like it was gonna most likely last forever.

But me, I was feelin' the approach of one of them bleak moods where I know I ain't.

Matt was flopped down in a country sprawl, one foot up on the dashboard and the other pulled up across his knee. With green eyes and that long blond hair of his he had the natural and common beauty of the American heritage thrown to and blowin' in the wind. His jeans was stretched tight across his thighs and butt makin' those sexy lookin' rolls and tucks around the crotch and fly that I like so much the look of.

I was watchin' him watch the dust blow across the road.

"You a virgin, Matt?" I said.

"No."

"How long's it been since you ain't?"

"Oh, about two years."

I leaned back in the seat, my hat comin' down low on my eyes.

"So when'd you last get a piece?" I said.

"Aw shit, Makon... "

"C'mon, tell me."

The boy was silent for a moment.

"Well," he said, "it was at that big Grange auction they had over at Hanson's Creek."

"Hell, that was almost three months ago! I was there but I sure didn't see you or anybody who looked like you."

Matt blushed, and I knew then he was lyin'.

"Well hell, Makon," he said testily, "you gonna tell me you're doin' any better?"

"Oh, a little."

I made a small laugh for effect.

"Man," I said, "I bet you beat off a lot durin' these long dry spells you seem to have."

"Yeah, some. Sure. And I suppose you don't, huh? And besides, what of it if I do?"

"Nothin'. Nothin' at all. 'Course there ain't no real need for it is all. Shit, I mean a guy can find other ways of gettin' his nuts popped other'n that. Although, mind you, I sure ain't got nothin' against jackin' off."

Matt was quiet for a moment.

"Just what *other* ways do you mean?" he said.

100

THREE: "Bridges"

I could sense a tightenin' in his mood, sorta like he was waitin' for somethin' to happen, somethin' that he knew to be truly needed and that he, even without utterin' the words, wanted.

"Well, it's like this," I said. "Sometimes certain men find ways of workin' things out between themselves."

"And how do they do that?"

"Oh, they get close."

"Close!"

"Yeah. They get closer than even friends."

Matt dropped his feet to the floor, crossin' his arms as if he meant to wait forever on whatever it was he figgered he might have to wait on.

I paused a minute and then said, "Would you say your dick's of a good size, Matt?"

"Well... yeah."

"You been circumcised?"

"No."

"You like it like that?"

"Yeah, I guess so." He laughed. "It looks good to *me* like that."

"They look good to me like that too."

My breathin' was gettin' kind of short. I had to use pretty good control in order to sound casual when I said, "And I'll just bet you're a real horny fella right now."

He sighed like he hurt in some way.

"Yeah," he said. "Kinda."

"Hell yes! A healthy fella your age needs relief every two or three days. You know that, don'tcha?"

He nodded.

"And it's a whole lot nicer havin' somebody else doin' the work. Thataway all you need to do is enjoy it."

He nodded again.

"Yeah," I said softly, "all you hafta do is lay back and enjoy."

I put my hand on his knee, runnin' it a little way up his thigh.

"Oh boy," I said, "I bet you're a pistol when you get somethin' hot workin' on that meat of yours. Somethin' wet and hot and real smooth. Real smooth and nice."

"Oh Jesus," Matt breathed.

101

His thigh tensed, then relaxed as he went lower on the seat, his legs spreadin' wider. I put down a solid, encouragin' squeeze and that brought up a definite surge in his jeans.

"Oh yes, you're a hot boy," I said. "I can see that."

"Yeah, I guess so."

"You know I can help you out, don'tcha?"

"Yeah?"

His voice was growin' raspy, urgent.

"Why, sure," I said.

"Well... how?"

"By doin' what I like to do."

I put my hand on his crotch. I could feel the restless hardness there, and it felt good.

"It's a nice, warm feelin' you get in what I do," I said. "You'd sure like it, I know that."

His legs spread even wider and his hands fell to his sides as if givin' permission.

"It's warm and easy, Matt," I said softly, coaxin'ly. "All you hafta do is enjoy it."

He lay his head back on the seat.

"You bet," I murmured. "All you hafta to is enjoy. Nothin' else. There's nothin' to it."

My fingers movin' in nimble authority, I opened his belt, popped the buttons of his jeans, and laid open the fly. In the gathered bunchiness of white boxer shorts I could see the cock bein' held there in tight, curved restraint. I had to work a little at findin' the gap.

"Raise up your hips," I whispered.

When he made that short effort I moved fast to pull jeans and shorts past his butt to mid-thigh. His cock sprung up in the fleshy grandeur of an indolent prince, the head glowin' from pink to peach as it emerged from its private seclusion beneath the satiny ruff of a luxuriant foreskin. Smirkin' in a red sass, the slit seeped those silvery drops so intricate in the design of this ever compellin' enterprise. Always eager I was summoned once again to the celebration of suck. Takin' his balls in hand, their soft, limited mobility warm with promise, I moved onto the curvin' knob, its sleek form well fitted to the reception to be found in my mouth.

"Oh for the crucifixion of Christ," Matt whispered, "that feels good, Makon. Oh goddammit!"

Gently provoked by the clamor bein' heated in that penis, I sent my tongue in a flat curl around the head, plyin' the tender nut with wet caresses and bouncy punches that rolled into long, slick licks. Then sealin' my lips around the shaft, I made tight turns in the downward movement as I went to the root of the cock connectin' me to this wonderful and so very, very American boy.

"Oh Makon," he groaned, his body turnin' in small twists against the tension he was feelin', and that I was helpin' so mightily to build.

"Makon! Oh fuckin' Jesus!"

The organ was growin' fat toward the threat of response so I came off it but kept the beat goin' with the slow and steady grip of my hand. My mouth, forever at a hunger for new adventure, went to his nuts to kiss, lick, nuzzle, lap, and suck. High up and back between his thighs and just beyond the folded corridor lay the anal rose, furled tight, its warm aroma of boyhood reachin' my nostrils now pressed low into the healthy sag of his scrotum.

"Goddammit, Makon! Jesus, I'm gonna shoot a wad in just a fuckin' minute."

I pulled back and looked up into his angelic face, now full with the enthusiasm of a young man runnin' at a stiff pace with his very natural urges of his very natural body. I held his cock in my hand, the push of his youth pushin' it at me. I rolled it in a smooth jack off.

"So then, Matt," I said, "you like this okay?"

"Shit, man, it's bein' nasty like I ain't never been before. It's like bein' pissed on... by God."

Whoa!

Well, I thought in a hot, silky gloat, there might be definite possibilities residin' here in this boy.

And so feelin' affirmed in expectation and with hazy flowers of the future bloomin' in my mind, I returned to the comfortable suck. I made a channel of my lips and tongue and went down on his stiff meat with the dedication of a philanderer ordained in sleaze, the fancy getup of the gig bein' a robe trimmed out in a deep shade of lavender that draped nicely across my shoulders. Wheelin' away on that dick I called on all my able

103

abilities as a cocksucker to haul Matt up to the threshold of the jump into the fringes of paradise. Well-timed and consistent, those efforts grew steadily in tempo as Matt, so keen for his go in the slippery slot, entered into the slidin' exchange. Pushin' and turnin' his hips in the ancient, liquid quest, he helped in bringin' the organ once again close to its angry condition of spit. The head swollen, it was gettin' ready to launch the sticky drench into my mouth. I closed my eyes as I prepared for the lovely slaps of hot jizz.

I felt a hand fumblin' at the tight, strainin' bulge in my jeans.

"Shit, man," Matt muttered, "I just gotta see your dick. I just gotta get a look at your dick. And touch it."

The fella was takin' another step into my world, and though I wasn't dismayed, it was a little bit faster than I'd expected.

Obligin' as always, I flipped the buttons and pushed open the fly.

Bein' as I ain't given to the convention of underwear, my cock, a giant thing hung with nuts of heroic size, bound into the arena with all its flags fully strung up and flyin' with the stiff optimism to be found in a robust libido. I was flooded with warm confidence in havin' such a manly presence, and when Matt's hand, cool and hesitant, closed on the burnin' staff most of that warmth coursed into my belly and down through my legs. It spun in my asshole. My balls, so thickly and stupidly eager, turned in a simple-minded joy.

"Jesus Christ," Matt murmured, "it ain't even a horse that's got anythin' like that."

His hand moved on it and took it into a staggerin' pump that moved fast toward the clutch of possession. His cock was deep in my throat, poised there in arrested motion as I awaited the ascension of the hellish essence. For that moment the crest denied, I came up to torture the slit in a mean, between-the-legs kinda love. My urge was now leadin' me into the prickly garden of greed, and in that angular place, with high limbs hung with heavy, slick, brown seeds, I licked my fingers and went between the boy's buttocks. Findin' the spot, its round, cushy bow prim in oblivion, I pushed in, goin' fast for the plunder to be found in surprise. His cock jumped into a paroxysm of witless frenzy. I moved quickly to quell that jerkin' with deep plunges of steady, serious suckin' while my finger persisted in its turnin' in the earthy hole.

"Oh, goddammit," Matt muttered.

And then a moan came from deep within his body, very likely thrown up from his soul.

"I'm gonna fuckin' come, Makon."

Oh God, I was on the very threshold of that twisted, miraculous ecstasy found in the zeal and the squeal of the squirtin' of the manly stuff. Saturated with the licentious, bent into the lewd, I adored the thick, loose chains of jizz that were delivered out of Matt's cock, thick spurt by thick spurt, into my mouth. Collectin' on my tongue, drippin' from my lips, the mess seeped back into my throat forcin' me into a gulpin' swallow. Oh shit, man, I was sunk in the deepest swill of joy as that handsome American boy popped his wad in my mouth.

"Oh boy. *Oh* fuckin' boy," Matt gasped softly, his body now spread low and spent. "Whew, that was sure somethin' all right. Jesus Christ, I'm all done in."

"That's good, kiddo," I said, "but we ain't quite done yet. Now maybe you could lend a hand and jack me off."

My voice was perfunctory in the simplicity of the demand for I stood girded now in authority, and a certain regal decadence, on the very summit of the most sublime of destructions. I was the guy who hadn't come yet. But Matt was not at all reluctant to join in. His hands, ambitious in a double clutch, moved into the labor, and in a sprint of immediate seconds a great, awesome—even to me after all this time—pitch of jizz sailed out of my cock in a flight toward the dusty, saggin' headliner above us. Two salvos hit it, a third fell short and smacked down on the radio. Those followin', in their customary ooze, sank back on the staff, drippin' down, fallin' away like the jewels of a broken diadem. Oh God, red and pink and sloppy as all get out, the thing was a picture of stunnin', intimidatin' maleness, and I loved it.

"Jesus," Matt said softly, dreamily, caught up in our filmy ruse, "I ain't never seen nothin' like that before."

"Does it every time," I said, feelin' a stretch of pride in my chest. "Yeah. And God, it *really* pops off if there's somebody nice—well, somebody like you for instance—fuckin' me up the ass."

"Yeah? Fuckin' you up the ass?"

"That's right."

105

"I don't believe it."

"It's true."

The boy looked up at the roof as if considerin' some point of philosophical nicety.

"You can take a cock up the ass, huh?" he said. "A pretty big one?"

"Sure. Wantin' to and knowin' how to do it right is what's important and makes it nice."

Matt frowned.

And then he looked at me with lascivious interest, a wicked leer washin' across his Sunday school face.

"Would that fuckin' be somethin' at guy might expect to happen on a regular basis?" he said.

"I expect so. And there could be blowjobs too."

"And blowjobs too, huh?"

I nodded.

Matt grinned as if he'd heard somebody dignified and important, like God Almighty Himself, lay out a long, loud fart.

"I'll be a sonuvabitch," he said.

I straightened my pants and started puttin' things away.

"Hey!"

It was a voice from outside our bastion of privacy.

"Hey! Hey there, you guys there in that pickup. Is that you, Matt?"

Matt rose up and looked out the back window.

"Oh golly, it's Roy," he said, "and he's got my package, sure enough. Oh boy!"

Pullin' his pants together Matt hopped out of the pickup to go collect his package from Roy the mailman.

Well, what could I really expect? A confession of love, an announcement of undyin' devotion, and a whole hill of promises? Dammit, I'm no dumbbell. The fellow was young and, of course, horny. I'd actually shown him what I had to offer and he'd taken a sample and liked it. And now his goddamned package, the one he'd been lookin' for in the first place, had arrived. But more important than any package, what I had offered him was adventure, which you don't get in any mail order deal, and *that* only in the beginnin' ways.

He'd be back.

And he was.

And pretty quick too.

Well, I didn't set out to get a hot, flamin' romance and that's just what I didn't get.

But what I did get was a friendship with a handsome young man who, like me, was of limited education but in possession of an inquirin' and open mind. Well, his sexual ardor didn't burn with the same hot coals that I stoked in mine, and his kinks weren't always as deep or as tight, or bent in the same direction as mine, but he never seemed to find, or needed to find, anythin' about me that wasn't okay enough to accept in a friend. I was happy with the way things went along and Matt seemed satisfied too.

A little later on, not too long after Labor Day, there was a fire at Matt's place. His grandpa had fell asleep with a pot of beans on the hot plate. They burned dry and then the heat got to the curtains and soon the flames found a stack of newspapers. In hardly no time a good part of the shack went up. They found the old man in his chair in the corner by his radio. He'd been caught by the smoke.

I drove out there that afternoon after the burial.

"I hate this fuckin' place," Matt said. "It's miserable and dirty, and most of the time it stinks."

He'd built himself a sort of lean-to affair across the unburnt part of the shack. If the winter winds came up from the south, which they don't, it might've been all right.

I stood leanin' against the pickup. I nodded at some boxes, bound up with wire, stacked in the back.

"I'm pullin' out," I said.

"Yeah? Where to?"

"San Francisco, California."

"Oh man! No shit?"

"No shit," I replied.

I saw, as I'd expected, a shinin' hope in his eyes, and then that was followed by a quiet, dignified desperation.

I put my hand on his shoulder.

"C'mon, Matt," I said, "and go with me."

"Aw, shit, I ain't got nothin'... "

I nodded.

"That's true all right," I said. "There ain't one fuckin' thing you got here. All I see is high rent due on a sorry, burnt out shack."

Then Matt smiled, possibility growin' toward reality in the simplicity of those given to faith.

"If I only could, though," he sighed. "God, at last I'd get a chance to see them bridges."

"And there's others out there too. Others besides them two."

"Well, maybe, but of all those I know of in the whole world... "

"Yeah, I know, they're in San Francisco." I paused. "C'mon and go with me, Matt. I can take care of things for both of us. There ain't much we need. Not right off. We can get work. C'mon and go with me."

Matt looked at me squarely. "Are you really sure, Makon?"

"I wouldn't be askin' if I wasn't."

He cast a glance at the shack where the black plastic was billowin' in the wind.

"Okay," he said.

So, abidin' by an American tradition spannin' four centuries we just picked up and moved on. But it wasn't as precarious as it sounds. Though battered, the pickup was recently tuned-up and ran well, the tires were in good shape, and I had insurance at an adequate coverage. So? Also, I had a little money, my health, several decades left of reasonably good expectation, and, probably for a little while at least, Matt. So? Also, I'd been to San Francisco before. I knew my way around, well, somewhat, and, perhaps, some people.

So?

So we just up and took off.

When Matt first saw the bridges I thought he was gonna cry. By God, I never saw a boy with such open-hearted dedication to somethin' that wouldn't never give back one thing even if it could. He was put into a near epiphany when we actually drove over the Bay Bridge with the Golden Gate in full view across the water and serenely majestic above the billowin' banks of slow movin' fog.

"Jesus, Makon," he said almost breathlessly, "I can't believe I'm really here where people live every day in the presence of these heavenly beauties, these heavenly, earthbound beauties."

He looked at me and smiled.

So, our days in San Francisco got off to a good start. We got us a motel, found a few places to eat at that had some decent food for affordable prices, and started layin' down, day by day, the foundations for a new life. I got a job drivin' a truck for a big printin' outfit. It was kinda hard at first bein' the city'd changed some, but with a map I got along okay. I bought a few things, clothes for Matt mainly, and then a VCR and some other stuff to sorta put us a home together.

After maybe two weeks and we were pretty well set up—I don't like to just blow into town and call someone—I decided it was time to get in touch with Will Brubaker.

"Yeah, it's me," I said on the phone. "Yeah! Right here in San Francisco. Oh, I don't know, just a few weeks. Sure. Tomorrow night? Sure. I'll bring Matt. Sure. You'll like him. Same place? Yeah. 'Bye."

That evenin' when I was finishin' up in the shower Matt came in lookin' happy and pleased as if he'd just scored a hot deal on some high priced real estate. He was takin' well to the hustle and bustle of city life bein' as he was of a nature basically optimistic. He looked very fetchin' standin' there in a pair of tan trousers and a brown polo shirt I'd picked out for him.

He was watchin' me in the mirror.

"Guess what," he said.

"I guess."

"No. Guess."

I shrugged.

"I guess," I said, "that you want to go back home."

"No! Hell no! I got a job."

"Well, by God, Matt, that's great. What kinda job is it?"

He smiled. "You'd never guess."

"Well, that's what I figured."

"I'm gonna be helpin' put up billboard signs all over this wonderful city. I mean big billboards too!"

He was beamin' with pleasure.

"Well, pal," I said, "I'm proud of you. Dammit, I'm really proud."

And I was.

He stepped up behind me keepin' his eyes on mine. His hands went across my chest, down my belly to my crotch. His fingers worked small tickles against my cock and balls. A hard-on was comin' up at a good, healthy clip.

"Makon, I owe you more than anything I could ever pay."

I shook my head.

"You don't owe me one thing, Matt."

"Well then, I'll just take somethin' for myself."

He went to his knees.

"Turn around," he said. "I'm gonna suck you off."

Already in an agitated state, my cock fairly leaped to a full erection as that candid young fella took my balls in one hand and, with the other far back on the shaft, began suckin' on the head. Though as yet unseasoned in the nuances of the effort, he was direct and resolute in his tight and not always gentle turns and twists as he set into motion a blowjob that was as unadorned as any staged in the raunchiest of toilets. Spreadin' my feet in the cocky stance of the days of Hong Kong trade I leaned back to let the boy show his stuff as the ever-envelopin' arms of that fatuous goddess workin' the game took over and led me once again into the convoluted, curious miracle. Matt's suckin' was good, his devotion to it evidence of yet another life to be laid at that maligned altar where I, in my draggy duds as an elder, began helpin' the worship along with sharp thrusts forward. And soon enough the pinpricks announcin' the comin' celebration danced down through my dick to my nuts. My asshole, so often a throne to seat a visitin' dignitary, lay coiled in alerted expectation. When a thumb, hooked back, made its probin' entrance the coil loosed itself and clamped down like a greedy viper.

"Oh Jesus," I moaned. "Yeah, baby, thumb fuck me."

Now suckin' with the exalted of all our history, Matt ran the turns on me. His thumb, growin' slick with the juices it made flow, was joined by a finger, and then two were hitched into the race ridin' in a neat little buggy of sweet pain. Bein' yanked up tighter and tighter toward the finish I moved down into a shallow squat, my asshole hot on Matt's fingers.

"It's comin', honey!" I shouted.

His lips at the head of my cock, Matt looked up and flashed me a lewd, knowin' glance. The healthy openness of his handsome face then distorted with the slickest and sloppiest of slapped-down-on-a-wet-concrete-floor passion pulled the trip line in my nuts.

I groaned.

"Oh you got it, baby."

The stuff, the grease, the gall and the gang of it, came up from that black well, spinnin' in the mighty, magical curse to slam into Matt's fabulously perfect mouth. He took it solid and still, and then moved in a soothin' sway while the jerkin' and pushin' were laid away into history. Pullin' his fingers from my butt he moved back to sit on his haunches.

"God," he said in a wide grin, "that thing always shoots like a cannon no matter where you aim it."

I laughed and reached down to pull him up.

"C'mon, hot stuff," I said, "I'll wash your back."

"You know," he said when he stood, "I'm gonna get fucked by that thing some day and it's gonna be soon."

"Okay, and believe me I'm lookin' forward to it but now let's see you in the shower."

While I got the water adjusted he stripped down. Turnin' to me, his dick swingin' in stiff, waitin' arcs, I was overwhelmed by a need to succor him in sex but also to nurture and protect him. But in the need of the immediate matter I directed him into the shower and followed.

Soapin' his body under the gentle spray, my hands sailed on his shoulders, went down his arms and worked across his chest feelin' the pecs shaped like smooth tropical fruits growin' slowly ripe in the long days of hot sun. Then movin' down over the belly to his penis and scrotum, I went between his thighs to the crease. Tucked within, the asshole was wet, slick, and nicely tight, and was now made even more tantalizin' by the challenge of an imminent, if indefinite, gratification. Returnin' to the cock strainin' at its leash of pent-up energy I began a steady, relentless, controlled, and slow jack off as if I'd been sent there as a heavenly torturer. Lickin', kissin', and puttin' small bites on his neck and shoulders I rolled his body, young and firm, vital and trustin', against mine, a muscular haven fully capable of delivering a crush of love.

"Jesus, Makon," he whispered, "the bird's gonna fly."

"Let it fly, baby."

"Oh shit, it's gonna fly."

"Let it fly, baby."

My cock, once again erected, danced in lewd grandeur near its prize—

seekin' just the lightest passin' kiss—as the shimmerin' young fella in my arms stiffened and let fly a hot wad of spit from the bird I held carefully caged in my hand.

I was lyin' on our tank of a motel bed when Matt came out of the bathroom lookin' like the cleanest of all queens' consorts. He sat down and kissed me on the belly.

"Well, now," I said, "I've got somethin' to tell *you*."

He gleamed with expectation.

"We're goin' out to dinner tomorrow night, and I don't mean no cheap cafe. We're gonna have us a fine dinner with Will Brubaker."

Matt's eyes clouded as if perceivin' a threat.

"Who's Will Brubaker?" he said in a low voice.

"Oh, Will and I go back quite a few years to the days of... Oh, hell, Will's an old friend livin' right here in San Francisco. I called him up this mornin' and he asked us to come over for dinner."

"I ain't gonna be in the way, am I?"

"Oh hell no. I know you're gonna like him. He's a great guy. And I know he's gonna love you."

"Okay."

"And you'll be able to see the bridges as you have never seen any bridges before. Will's house is way up there on Telegraph Hill."

Matt nodded, a certain diffidence in his manner.

Well, history is writ, but I suppose if there hadn't been such a wanderin' lust in my restless soul Will Brubaker and I could have made somethin' together. I don't know. But the real truth was that while I was livin' my nomadic life from palm tree to icy hill, Will was puttin' in eighteen hour days and seven day weeks buildin' his importin' business known as GeeGaw Collections International. But, you know, he never seemed to resent my poppin' up every now and then, and stayin' a while and then... hell, who doesn't know the pattern. And here I was about to do it again, but this time I felt a different man, and that in so many, many different ways. I felt neither threatened nor a threat.

So the next evenin' we walked up the steep, narrow walk to the old Victorian house that, when I actually saw it, I remembered in greater detail than I'd expected. The paint maybe seemed in better condition or the plants better cared for—I don't know, it was all just *prettier*—and so the place, somehow, didn't look so imposin' or seem so important in the ways in the past that had always been so far beyond me.

I rang the bell.

"Nice house," Matt said nervously.

"Big."

"Yeah."

"Is that you, Makon?"

That familiar, mellow voice came from above. I stepped back and looked up. It was of course Will.

"Yes, by God," he exclaimed. "It *is* you!"

"Yep, it's me all right."

"Don't move! I'll be right down."

Soon enough the tall door glided open and Will Brubaker stood there grinnin' the widest welcome in the world. He'd gone gray some, but the sturdy, steady man of strong commitment stood there in the lanky posture I'd always found so attractive.

"Makon! Goddammit, it's so good to see you!" His dark eyes gleamed with pleasure.

"Jesus Christ, Will," I said, "it's so damned good to see you. You look good. Hell, you look great!"

"Well... "

Our embrace was brief but in no way superficial or awkward, and then I introduced Matt and Will. They shook hands and we moved on into the house.

As it always had been—and now even more so in these times of growin' sophistication—it was a show-stopper of taste and elegance. But Matt went immediately to the wide windows overlookin' the city and the bay. The bridges glowed in the last rays of the settin' sun, their towers magnificent in permanence and purpose. Glancin' at me Will approached the window and stood at Matt's side, the two in a silent gaze upon the might wrought by the hands of men. In a placid greetin' Will's arm went around the young fellow's shoulder. Matt looked up smilin' in a satisfied calm.

"By God, those bridges are the most beautiful creations on earth," he said softly.

"Do you like San Francisco, Matt?"

"Oh yes sir," he replied. "I sure do even though it's only a few weeks we been here."

"Think you'll stay?"

Matt's answer came quick, without hesitation.

"Oh yes," he replied. "And I know I'll never get tired of lookin' at those bridges out there."

The view was as commandin' as it ever was, but now it's perspective seemed less narrow to me, less constrictive.

I walked closer.

"Matt can tell you more about those bridges, and about a hundred others, than any man anywhere."

"Is that so," Will said.

He stood away, his benignly handsome face glowin' softly as he gazed on Matt's flushed countenance.

"That's right," I said, "Matt's a bridge expert."

"Aw, for God's sake, Makon," Matt said.

"The hell!"

Matt looked at Will with a disarmin'ly embarrassed charm.

"Well," Will said, "let's sit down for a while and talk. Dinner's doing its thing in the oven."

Matt sat down in a luxurious Scandinavian chair and looked around in frank interest. And then movin' back, he nodded his head in approval. In just a little while the conversation was goin' along at a comfortable clip and Matt was helpin' Will in the passin' of soft drinks and small edibles.

Pretty soon we heard a bell ringin' from the kitchen.

"It's ready," Will said. "We've got meat and potatoes, plus a few other oddball things."

And it was a fine meal. The roast beef was put out with an overflowin' abundance of the freshest and finest vegetables I'd seen since departin' for the romance of desert livin'. Matt's eyes were as big as his plate—bigger, as he worked his way through two helpin's. There were assortments of imported specialties and condiments, and that famous San Francisco sourdough bread with sweet butter. Followin' all that was a tall layer cake and two kinds of pie, and ice cream rich enough to float on.

Afterward we sat around the table for a long time just talkin'. We touched on old times, the new times, and the future. We felt happy, sad, nostalgic, and glad that we were alive and could share that life in health and relative wealth.

After the fairly heavy stuff was over, Matt and Will fell into a banterin' and easy goin' friendship.

Along about eleven I stood up to start the wheels rollin' for our departure.

"Well, Will, we gotta go," I said. "You see, Matt here is startin' his new job tomorrow."

"Is that so?" Will said. "Where?"

"At Outdoor Festival Signs," Matt replied.

"Oh I know that," Will said. "My new office is not more than two blocks away."

"Over by those big tanks near the airport?" Matt asked.

"That's it," Will said. He fiddled a little with the clutter on the table. "Why don't you two stay over. We shouldn't have any problem seeing to it that Matt gets to work on time."

Matt looked at Will then at me. "Do you want to Makon?"

"Do you?"

Matt's eyes were bright.

"Yes."

"Then I don't see why not!"

In a big bedroom at the head of the stairs Will set about gettin' things ready for us. He put out towels, tooth brushes, and pajamas. When turnin' down the bed he fluffed up that luxurious beddin' I'd forgotten he had such an self-indulgent preference for. I was workin' slowly at the buttons of my shirt watchin' the man's confident movements, so characteristic of his gentle, purposeful disposition. Memories of peaceful nights—and many ridden with hot passion—moved those bawdy impulses I always carry in my pants. I felt like a poor cousin suddenly rich.

"Oh God, Makon," Will said, his voice goin' kinda hoarse, "it's so nice seeing you in this house again."

"I'm glad I called."

"I am too. You and Matt will always be welcome here."

Matt came out of the bathroom with his white boxers hangin' low at his slim hips in a way that wrapped that hard little body in a licentious invitation. I followed Will's gaze, calm in discreet desire, as it followed the young man as he circled the bed and then jumped onto it. Settlin' in and in that resolute way of his, Matt crossed his legs like he was quite willin' to sit there and wait—and for as long as necessary too—on any new developments that might be comin' his way.

He put his hands on his knees.

"Well, by God," he said, "it sure enough looks to me like you guys belonged together."

I looked away, small guilts tuggin' at my heart.

"We did have certain rapport," Will murmured, lookin' at me. "And I still have a big piece of it."

I looked back at Will.

"And," I replied, "I'd be lyin' if I said I didn't."

"Well, what the hell," Matt said. "C'mon, then. Jesus, what could be righter. I'm excited as all hell!"

Throwin' off his shirt and droppin' his pants, Will's reserve hit the carpet just as fast his clothes did. He slid onto the bed where he lay waitin' in poised expectation, his slender body sleek and firm from the years of methodical attention.

Well, with such tantalizations awaitin' I made short work of doffin' my own duds.

I lay down on the bed, Matt between me and Will.

"Jesus Christ!" Matt exclaimed. "I gotta be the luckiest guy in San Francisco. Look! Just look, I got me two of the tallest, good-lookin'est men in this whole city without knowin' how I did it, and to boot I don't even know what's gonna happen."

I put my hand on Matt's knee.

"Kiddo," I said, "there ain't nothin' gonna happen that no one wants to happen. Ain't that right, Will?"

"That's right."

Matt, bein' master of his own ship, seemed satisfied with that and went right away to a crouch before Will. The man's trim pale blue designer underwear were at a listin' bulge, the marvelous sag goin' off down his leg. With Matt's slightest tug the frail elastic gave way and Will's fine cock reared up into his face. The head, circumcised, had the comely countenance of a creature well aware of the depth of its beauty and, jerkin' in humpin' spasms of greetin', its mouth oozed with the silvery, slippery slop. Matt toyed with it in indolent decadence, thumb, forefinger, and cockhead in a tight ballet that drew small groans of pleasure from Will.

"I always liked the look of this stuff," Matt said softly. "I never did know if anybody had it besides me."

"We've all got it, Matt," Will said.

"Yeah, I know that now. It sure is neat. I love men stuff."

Then the fair fella, yet new in the ancient endeavor, put his mouth on that dilly of a dong and began the suckin' plunges, one after another, in the very finest form of all our cocksuckin' elite. That put his ass out there for the mountin' of another neat perversion so I, also in a crouch, moved down intent on the suckin' of asshole. I pushed the cheeks apart with my fingers and entered the crease. The rubbery goodness met me with a prim pucker and a sweet wink as my tongue, wide and lovin'ly wet, launched another fine vessel into these fascinatin' seas of debauchery. Suckin' his asshole knowin' that he was suckin' the dick I'd sucked many a time in pits of passion and flights of love, I was twisted into a wonderful desire for all of everythin' good for everyone. I came up on my haunches with my dick thrust out in its usual impudent status of excess.

With it in my hand, I looked upon the compact body before me and said, "I'm gonna be fuckin' you, Matt."

"Oh Jesus," Will murmured, his eyes glitterin' with a certain kind of brittle, ever-increasin' joy.

"I'm gonna fuck you, Matt-boy," I repeated. "You hear me?"

Matt came up from Will's cock. There was a wicked smile pulled across his pretty, wet mouth.

"I heard," he said. "And it ain't gonna be none too soon neither."

After layin' a thick spread of grease on Matt's bung Will handed me the tube then opened wide his own legs wide to give Matt all possible comfort in his suckin' as we moved toward the rack of the enchantin' masculine torture soon comin' up. With a hand on Matt's shoulder I laid my dick, greasy and grand, at the portal of the consumin' desire that is born of no less than the push of life itself. The knob a greedy, horny red at a fully gross distention, I pushed against the tight clutch, at once exhilarated and damned, the exhilaration seated in the sharin', the damnation lyin' in its brevity. The rubbery ring, so simple and so marvelous, resisted for a few heavy seconds only, and then—flexibility numberin' among its many

117

charms—it lay itself open in submissive glory and then began suckin' in the tube by the fractional inches.

Matt's bobbin' head slowed down to a near stop.

"Does that hurt, honey?" I said.

Matt's head then came up.

"Oh God," he said. "It hurts like a Mack truck goin' up my butt."

"Well put," Will observed.

"Do you want to stop?" I said.

"No!"

With most of any possible alarm now at bay but caution still the watchword, I pushed on findin' the old thrill ever new as the tight constrictions of this boy's sweet anus worked slowly along the shaft until my thighs kissed at his. God, it was perfect! And then puttin' my hand under his belly I found the prod there hard, heavy, and meaty, and seekin' somethin' dandy—and handy—for itself.

"How are you doin', Will?" I asked.

"Hell, I'm close to a blast right now!"

"Hold on there, old buddy. In just a little bit now we'll get Matt into you, and then we'll all go for a nice ride."

"You bet. I'm right with you."

Its authority soon established in the lovely labor at hand, my meat, that probin' blood-filled prong of diligent effort, moved into a round of long, steady strokes of serene confidence. The bond of trust we had in place was now extended in those heavenly movements—the symphony of cornholin'—into the indefinite future. I was the guy of guys—yeah, all gay guys everywhere—gifted in the givin' and gettin' of the magic that this manly and very exclusive pursuit bestows.

"Are you okay, Matt?" Will asked.

The boy came up on his elbows. "Oh God, I'm bein' *pushed* into some screwball kinda heaven without even havin' to ask."

He looked over his shoulder at me and winked, and then quickly back at Will.

"Come give me a kiss, Will," he said.

Movin' to their knees, my two friends—so different and yet so the same—fell into a long and fervent kiss, their very simpatico embrace bein' fueled by the rugged work bein' done by my cock. And in that work I was granted a power of the most approachable kind in a world rife with its distorted perception. I was granted the power of love in all its frustratin' and edgy—and lovely—confusions. Through my asshole love sang songs of sly lust and silly madrigals of happy, peekaboo deceptions of warm summer evenin's.

At the endin' of their kiss Will brushed a light caress on my cheek and bent into a fuckable crouch in front of Matt. His butt, boyish and yet slung with the baggage of survival, called loud and clear for an invasion of the anus winking its coy leave there between the fleshy globes. New to this but no clown, Matt saw the invitation and we, in an ad-libbed shuffle, moved toward the waitin' Will and his well-greased asshole. With me in full penetration Matt sank into Will with the acolytic radiance of an innocent renegade stridin' manfully into his own inevitable future of disrepute. Grapplin' for a moment with the timin', soon enough he had the wheel of the fuck well in hand and we moved at a rapid pace into the refined world of the double fuck.

"Man oh man!" Matt exclaimed hoarsely. "Ain't this just the fuckin' fuck of heaven!" He giggled. "And with all manner of horny holy hosts lookin' on for Christ's sake!"

"Oh Matt, baby," Will crooned. "Oh my God, you sweet young creature, fuck me!"

So we rolled along, we three, bound up in the peachy chains of lust that clinked with wonderful sounds as we dragged them behind us in a carpet of flowers. Matt was exemplary in the cadence maintained, Will was his steady, reliable self handsomely spread out with his asshole hostin' the star of this willin'ly wicked constellation of gay fellas, and I, well I, vain enough in pride to take credit for the sizable cock bein' thrust into Matt and the main engine in this petite extravaganza of lust, felt the poetry of the outrageous, the common, and the quaint spinnin' in my head. My cock was servin' up just gobs of creamy sensation that dripped with the sticky sweets of lust, that lust hung on and in the bodies of these two wonderful fellas who tasted of bright red cherries saturated in sugar.

"Oh shit, Makon," Matt said softly. "I'm gonna come."

"Come, honey," I said.

"Yes, honey," sweet Will said, "come if you want."

"Shit, I can't not!"

The boy was in masterful control of himself, admirably so, right up to the explosion. But then some real verbal shit hit the fan. Oh God, he let fly with a litany of quaint obscenity that did more justice to scatological literature than anything we were actually doin' to each other, but it sure was nice to hear as the foxy little dude from Nevada worked himself down to the wire in the double fuck.

"Nastyboy low ball Jesus pimps Holy Ghost fuckin' pigs. Lay the bastard deep go for a hot drip in ass fuckin' cheap bellhop slut. Piss shit up his nose. Pus in the preacher, gonna reacher, hot cold cocker, better knocker. Up the fuckin' ass."

Matt was slammin' into Will and pushin' back onto me, back and forth into a hellish seesaw of screamin', jizz-pullin', shit-kickin', suckin'-ass cacophony.

"O, God's mother, pregnant by a fish, ain't that caviar, don't she wish. Sit on a pole, pull on your joint, ain't even a soul, got no point."

Makin' one last whoppin' turn he made the magnificent heave.

"Hey, you guys!" he yelled. "It's the fuckin' drip of heaven comin' right up!"

Then, vain, profane, lovely, human, and funny, he slumped down on Will's back, a boy hugely spent and breathin' hard. My cock rose in him like an unyieldin' bird of gentle predation.

"Okay, Will," I said, "now come fuck me so's we can put these hot deposits we're carryin' where they belong."

"Oh you bet, Makon."

Pullin' away from Matt's cock—out it came with a lewd smack—Will came around behind me and, without a whole lot of ceremony, plugged into my asshole while I went on pushin' hard in Matt's butt who was now an exalted pawn bein' used in the steamy matter of two lecherous guys workin' together to get their rocks off. After some nice strokes in masterful form it wasn't much longer before Will opened up his final barrage on me, and bearin' down hard on the little doodad mechanisms inside me that make all this shit worthwhile cracked his nuts. In a silky hell of heaven I worshipped at the altar of Matt's sensational ass while Will, still slopped in the abundance of love, pulled out and, low on his hands and knees, threw sucks and licks at my asshole. Stiff and rubbery, weak and possessed of mighty strength, I was elevated to a fantastic heaven where I delivered into

Matt's body a mighty spew of jizzycum, the sticky stuff that somehow sometimes helps glue driftin' lives together.

We lay there for many long minutes, the flow of time caught in the kinks of the postcoital enigma. And then when collectin' ourselves there was a new awareness of each other that this unique—well, maybe not so unique—swing of perversion had brought to us. We were no longer the same congenial group of men who had climbed those stairs together. And even if nothin' ever went any further than this sloppy, steamy, wet moment we were all forever changed both individually and in our perceptions of each other. The fellas who toss the salad ain't always the same fellas who toss in the sheets.

Rollin' off the bed to his feet, Will bent and kissed Matt, then me, and padded away to the john. Matt came up close to me, pushed his marvelous arrangement of muscles and bones against my ribs. He breathed hot against my ear.

I put my arm around his shoulder.

"Do you think," he said softly, "all this might happen again?"

"I don't see why not."

"Good. I thought maybe it would but sometimes I need reassurance."

Matt laughed and jumped from the bed, and then turned back. "But it's true, I do."

I got up and we followed Will into the bath.

He stood at the long window runnin' the length of the narrow space.

The bridges, silently constant in another night of the thousands, held high their lights of endurin' promise.

"I see them every day," Will said, "and I still sometimes forget how important they are."

Matt rolled a soft grab across Will's butt.

I put arm across his shoulders.

"Well, when you come right down to it," Matt said, "them bridges out there ain't nothin' but big pieces of cold iron that's been put together from a plan. That don't make them any less beautiful, but it's true."

Will pulled away from the window and looked at Matt with a certain patient amusement.

"And it seems to me," Matt said with bright-eyed optimism, "that what we got right here is a hell of a lot more than that."

Then Will looked at me smiling and shaking his head.

"Get in the shower, kiddo," I said. "We'll show you lots of iron. And it'll be hot iron too!"

"And you can take that for a promise," Will said.

Well, we showered, and while doin' it we did a little more explorin' of various body parts of various bodies, and I was pleased with the way Matt went from me to Will and back with equal enthusiasm—liftin' here and strokin' there—in a way that pretty well demonstrated that there wasn't any of that business of anybody bein' his favorite fella.

After we'd toweled off Will handed us terrycloth robes—Matt's yellow and mine green—that just swallowed us up in wholesome luxury.

"Fabulous!" Matt cried.

"They're part of a new line," Will said. "From Pakistan. Made from the very best Ismeki cotton."

"From the Ismeki Valley?" Matt asked.

"Why yes," Will said. "Do you know of the Ismeki Valley?"

"Well, not very much," Matt said. "What I know is that they're putting up one of the highest single span bridges in the world over there. It's gonna go from a town called Istanburlbad over to a plateau where there's rich copper deposits but no easy way to get up to 'em unless they build a whole slew of tunnels. The bridge is gonna be faster and cheaper."

Will whistled. "Well, I'll be."

"I told you he was an expert," I said.

"So you did."

Matt's grin was embarrassed, but pleased.

Early the next morning we piled into Will's '72 VW—bought new by the way—and took Matt, excited as all get out, to work. His stride was confident as he walked into the big building housing Outdoor Festival Signs.

"I wouldn't expect that young man to be long in helping put up billboards," Will said.

"No."

Will started the car.

"Do you have time for coffee down by the wharves?" he said.

"I've got about an hour."

"Good enough."

We went to this ancient Chinese dive that Will had always found attractive—for the color, don'tcha know. I didn't like it then and I didn't this time.

We sat out on the deck. The sun was bright, the wind brisk with quick gusts tugging at the gaudy oriental lanterns and streamers.

"Will you be staying long, Makon?" Will asked.

"That's hard to say. I want to see that Matt gets set on a nice firm foundation and then... "

"Don't dance with me, Makon. The boy admires you. He likes you. He might even love you, but don't avoid your responsibilities by putting them on him. If you're planning to move on, just say so."

"What I was going to say was that I wanted to see Matt established— however he wants it—and then figure out what's best to do. What I mean is, he might not even want to be around me in a few months or so. Know what I mean?"

"Sorry, Makon, I didn't mean to jump on you, and yes, I know what you mean."

I gazed on the bay and the ships bound for far off places, those comin' from those places, and some just sittin' there in the water. They were just ships after all and not vessels of promise and adventure.

"I love Matt, Will," I said. "I want to do what's right by him. Whatever it might be. I want never to be a disappointment to him."

I looked at Will.

"Will you help me do that, Will?"

Solid, regular, responsible Will smiled.

"Well, Makon," he said, "I'll do whatever I can. I wouldn't want to see Matt disappointed either."

"Thanks, Will."

Well, we ate breakfast—or Will did, that godawful Goong Gow Chee egg and fish concoction he always liked so much—and then went back to the house where my truck was parked.

"I don't want to intrude, Makon," Will said, "but do you think you and Matt might be coming to dinner tonight?"

"Well, say, since it's Matt's first day on the job why don't we pick him up and eat out someplace. Make a little celebration of it. Matt's nuts about spaghetti. It'll be my treat."

"Sure. Shall I'll book a table at Corelli's?"

"Well, I wasn't thinkin' about a place quite so classy."

"Corelli's isn't what I'd call classy. It's nice, but not classy. Don't worry, I'll help with the check."

"No, get us that table at Corelli's," I said. "But it's still my treat."

"Okay."

I got into my truck and rolled down the window.

"There hasn't been much in Matt's life in the way of celebration," I said. "I don't want to go all mushy, but I think I—we—can help change that. Maybe in some way we can help him make the right choices so's he don't get off on the wrong foot. God, gay life seems so much more complicated these days."

"It is. Coming out of the closet, as an individual or as an entire sub-culture, isn't the easiest thing to do."

I smiled at Will's learned way is summin' up a situation. "I'll pick up Matt and we'll see you here, okay?"

"At about six?"

"Right."

Will waved and went up the walk and into the house.

I started the truck and drove toward the heart of the city and, as they always do, the bridges, first one and then the other, came into view. Seein' them I thought about Matt—like I will, probably, for the rest of my life— and his simple and steadfast faith in the rightness of things. He always believed in the buildin' of bridges, and most certainly he believed in the strength and purpose of bridges. And here we were, the three of us, venturin' into the very important enterprise of buildin' bridges of communication and feelin' and understandin' between us.

And, yeah, maybe even of love.

Well, there sure ain't never nothin' wrong with buildin' bridges between folks.

Especially gay folks.

FOUR

HAYRIDE SATURDAY NIGHT

Well, God.

This guy had his cock nearly halfway up my butt even before my pants were down to my ankles. Sure it was nice, but hell, man, I was still trying to get some class into my life.

"Jesus Christ, man," I said out loud, "don't you know anything about decorum?"

"Yeah," he said. "I know the sooner I fuck 'em, the sooner I de-core 'em. So how's zat?"

"Well, shit," I replied.

"That ain't no shit, man."

"Oh never mind."

But even with that though, his cock was beginning to feel pretty good, like it does when a guy knows what the thing is for. That is when you're talking in terms of butt fucking.

"Now, dammit," he said, "just hold still for a while."

I'd picked him up at Hominy Bob's, a place where I sometimes hang out and also where I used to work at, on the corner of Third and Chattanooga, where they got the best and biggest chili dogs in downtown. They're cheap too. Well anyway, he was leaning against one of the stand-up tables in the back patio having, I guess, a coke. You can't tell now that fat boy Nick, being so cheap, has done away with the bottles and now has just the paper cups... aw, but shit, who the hell cares about that because I don't the fuck work there any more you know. So fuck it. But this guy I picked up there—Tolliver was his name—looked good. His pants weren't too tight so that, in the way I figure, if there's something showing it's going to be way more than just a mouthful. And he showed all right. Shit, I've got guys who have on tight pants and showing a lot and you get them home to find out it isn't anything but a big pimple. I'm not hot to get fucked by any big pimples. So anyway, I walked up to him, this guy Tolliver, and looked right at his crotch and I said does he want to dance a little in the afternoon. I know if I was a pretty little fella like those hanging out on Clancy Street I couldn't come on that way. They have to be coy and cute. Wiggle their butts and take little steps, and still act like they don't think they're cute—oh my, haven't got any idea at all. Oh no.

Well, this Tolliver guy gave me the old once over and said sure, like I knew he would.

Since I'm a big fella and pretty good-looking too, so's I'm told anyhow, and built nice, I can get away all right with saying things straight out to the guys I want to make it with. I learnt that pretty much up front. Big guys can be direct. In fact, it's even expected of them. Otherwise they're thought to be pussies.

So then I said okay, man, let's split.

Say though, before I go on much further, I'd better right now and very clear say that I not making any pretense at being any real kind of writer. No siree. It's just that I was reading in one of the gay newspapers I pick up now and then about the need for more honest communication between common people. Well, I'm sure as hell common all right, just about as common as anybody's likely to be. And since I've never been afraid to tell the truth about myself, and since I've always been pretty good at using words to express my feelings, even very personal ones, I figured I might as well have a fling at establishing some of that communication. So, if you're reading this—whoever you might be—I hope you like it because, though I don't really know what I might tell, I do like telling it, and I especially like telling the dirty parts.

Well anyhow, now that I've sort of cleared things up there, I'll get on with it.

Let's see, now where was I...

Oh, yeah.

My place isn't real nifty considering some I've seen since I come over here, but it's still pretty nice what with that little fridge and the stove tucked in back there behind the toilet. When I showed up over here about a year ago, after my mom and the little kids burned up in the fire, I met up with Carlton, the guy who had the pad. We messed around together a couple of times but there wasn't much of anything in it because he had this little dick that was more like an underfed night crawler than anything else, and which, in the really worst part, popped off the wad in nothing flat. And *then* there wasn't much to *that* either. Just this little bitty squeak of stuff. Poor guy, when it come down to the brass tacks he didn't have much at all, but, God, he sure was good-looking. Gorgeous. Like some movie star. Anyway, as friends we got along okay so I moved in to help out with paying the rent. And then come to find out the dude was on parole and the dumshit hadn't met with his officer for a long time. Just a little while back he got picked up for some minor deal (actually it was shoplifting) and was showed the way right quick back to the slammer. Dumshit. Anyhow, that's how I got to have the pad to myself. It's hard coming up with the rent sometimes but it sure is neat just knowing I have a place to myself. Lord knows, it's loads better than anything I could've ever hoped to have back in Pea Ridge.

Loads better.

In case you're wondering, that's Pea Ridge, Kentucky I'm talking about.

So when me and this fella from Hominy Bob's got there, I was fiddling with the window shade to make it dim and sexy when he comes up behind me. He starts running his hands up and down my back. Pretty soon he had his hands on my belt, and then my pants were open and my underwear pushed down below my balls. In nothing flat he'd slicked up his dick with spit and was going into me just like that. It's nice to go fast but it don't have to be quite that fast. That's when I made that remark about decorum. I figure to try and show a little class even if it isn't anything more than a pass with a street trick.

Oh boy, but once that ole charlie's in there, though, I'm a real round-heeled dolly. And especially if a guy's got a big cock like this one did. I can get down there and wait on forever being plowed, because it's something I can do and do it good and get along with a certain kind of

127

pride doing it. Some guy back in Pea Ridge by the name of Dale Tobbs, a real looker although there never was much mutual regard between us, said once that I did it just like some old sow. Now I didn't like that one bit. Fucking is my talent and my passion, and I don't put up with no nasty cracks about it. I threw a punch at Dale for that one. Fucking got him too. He carried around a beaut of a black eye for a good week and a half.

Ha!

But being down on the floor with this guy, him with his hands on my butt and throwing in the beginnings of a good fuck, I felt good. Sometimes being fucked is like having something golden beyond any price you could ever hope to pay, and you got it just because you got the stuff to get it with. By that I'm referring to good looks and the equipment to go with them. It don't do to dwell on it, but I am good-looking. I've seen guys, especially since I come over here, who aren't and they don't get what I get. I'm not being boastful because there's nothing in that either, but I do feel good walking down the street knowing my pants are filled out good and I can wear my shirt unbuttoned to my belly without looking the fool.

"Why don'tcha take yer pants off," Tolliver said.

Since it was beginning to look like more than a quickie I did that and took off my shirt too, and then laid down on the floor on my back and got ready to put my legs up on his shoulders and take the meat in like that.

Of course, as you can see, I really go for all this now, and have for some time. Being queer, and being fucked as a queer by other queers as well as being a queer fucking queers has become a special identity to me, something I prize in a queer way. But it isn't a condition that I just opened up like some goddamned book, you know. But still it started simple enough I suppose. It was this oddball shit Bud Brinsky who'd come up to Pea Ridge just for a week in July that did it to me for the first time when I was only about eleven or so. He got my legs up on his shoulders because he said he wanted me to be like a woman. I didn't know much about being a woman and all, but it sounded all right at the time. Oh damn, but did it hurt! It was one big fucking dick that guy had, and what spit he used wasn't near enough. And he wouldn't let me get away. He fucking forced me. I soon forgot about being any kind of woman. All I knew was that I was taking a dick up my asshole, and that it hurt. But pretty soon, looking around the pain, I found the idea pretty attractive in a confused sort of way.

128

Anyhow, after it was all over—six minutes tops—and ole Bud Brinsky had run away like some old-time ridge bandit, there was jizz, mainly jizz, and some blood, not a lot, all on my butt, and, Christ, even if I didn't know for sure what the hell it was all about, I was still excited and felt in some way selected, if you get my meaning. Anyway, I certainly didn't have no quarrel at all with it happening then, nor do I now because it started me off on a whole life of learning about dicks and buttholes. What I didn't like remembering later on was that it was a creep like Bud Brinsky—a molester you can bet—who was on me and up my butt for the first time. I still can't figure why I let him do it because he wasn't all that much bigger than me, and he sure as hell wasn't at all good-looking, but... well... Of course, like I say, I didn't know a whole lot about it then. Later there was lots of other guys around and lots better ones too. Lots better. Like Mickey Delaney. And Marsh Walker. And Abe Reichaus. And like the three Mortensen brothers. Yeah! Those guys! Wow! After I'd had more experience about how to go about playing the fuck game, I got all three of them, one by one. No. No, that's not right. Stanley and Bobby Mortensen did it to me together—twice—and oh man, Bobby had an enormous dick, just fucking enormous! And when he cracked his nuts it was like he was blowing the top off a mountain. It was wonderful. And then later I sucked off Richard Mortensen, the youngest brother, maybe three times before I got things fixed around to where he finally fucked me. Richard was the prettiest of the bunch, the whole bunch, and he was real sweet. I still have special feelings for him. I think he had some queer inclinations rolling around inside.

So considering it all, it worked out good enough.

For Pea Ridge anyhow.

I can't complain.

So this Tolliver guy, feeling me, said, "Tommy told me you had a good body. Nice butt too."

"Yeah?"

"Yeah."

"He said you was a good fuck too."

"Yeah?"

"Yeah."

I have to be honest. That's what I like to hear. Tommy's a pretty influential guy in our area. Real hot too. Nice. We made it a couple of

129

times. It helps to know you're getting a good reputation—don't go with no dogs. The guy with me right then, he was okay too. Not real handsome, but a pretty sharp body, and, of course, he had that go-ahead-on-it size dick. Nice. So anyway, with my legs up on his shoulders he slipped the meat into me and, Jesus Christ, did it feel good as he started pushing up into me in a determined way, and I knew *he* knew what he was doing. You'd be surprised how many don't, or maybe you wouldn't. But when they do, that's what I meant when I wrote the part about making the golden purchase. It don't mean a lot if you chew on it, but it's kind of neat to think about sometimes. Like in poetry. You don't *always* have to dwell real hard on the meaning of things.

So then after we'd been fucking for a short time this guy did something that don't happen too often. He put his hands on the sides of my face and kissed me really hard and then went real slow into a french. I just wasn't expecting it because almost nobody—including me—usually kisses like that with a person being picked up off the street or such. Jesus, I felt like he'd slapped me, and peeking out from between us my dick jumped in a fast dance which he saw, and that made us both laugh. That helped a lot in getting me a little more off the edge of wariness. Well, actually, it did us both a lot of good because the fucking then started moving toward something more than just being a place to drop your rocks. There were more serious kisses, nice kisses, longer and a lot less self-conscious. Rolling in that good feeling I flashed back on how really bad, after I got accustomed to being fucked regularly, I used to want them, the kisses, without even being aware of it. Most of the time most of the guys didn't want any kissing. Oh, they wanted to fuck all right, but they wouldn't want much to do with kissing. Little Jerry Bozarth did though. But he was the sissy everyone else always laughed at. He talked funny, kind of hoity-toity. And for some reason his pants never did seem to fit right although he did have a cute butt. Oh yes, I screwed Jerry all right, but his ideas about fucking were more along the lines of playing house than balls out cornholing. Jerry wasn't much interested in jizz, or how to actually *get* it, and if *I* wanted to get *anything*—butthole tail *or* jizz—I had to talk nice and act like refinement was something a guy should aspire to.

Now, all this might be making Pea Ridge sound like a wonderful place, but to tell the truth it just sure as hell wasn't. In all *other* areas it was the shitty pits, and if my mom and the little kids hadn't died like they did you can bet the pimples on the pope's nose that I'd still be stuck there.

Now, how'd I get to be here?

Oh yeah, the kissing.

The guy—Tolliver—was doing it really nice, like he was getting into feeling the spirit of the moment. I wanted to tell him that, but I didn't really know how so I just touched him and ran my hands over his back and arms in hopes he liked it and understood. When he looked into my face like he was feeling the need to start another kiss, I smiled. He smiled back in a hesitant sort of way.

"Yeah, you're an okay guy," he said and went on with the kiss.

I was beginning to feel real good about the progress we were making, so I reached around and put a couple of fingers on his asshole, just a little bit so's not to pose a threat. It puckered in the way they do, so I knew that he liked it okay. So I played there, really wanting to push in, but I didn't. Just by waiting out on the edge you sometimes get more than you would by trying right off for the whole banana, and really often winding up with nothing much at all. With somebody you don't even half know it takes some guys—me included—a little time to get built up to making a new move. The fingers were doing the job, though, because he was kissing a whole lot freer, like he wasn't hardly thinking about it anymore. I was giving back just as I got, and then some. The boiling point would be coming up soon. He pulled back a ways so's he could get at my dick. He started to jack it off. There was a little slacking in his fucking as he licked around his mouth like he wanted to have it in there, but that's hard to do along with the act we already had underway. It's also not very conclusive. I smiled again, and I guess he thought he'd better kiss me again. Actually I didn't, but that was all right. Feeling that I knew him a little better now I figured I'd ask him did he like his tits pinched and such.

"Say, man," I said, "do you go for tit play?"

"Yeah," he said.

"Sort of tight, I mean, like hard?"

"Not too."

So I started doing that but taking care not to go overboard. Some guys do that to me and I start to thinking more about what's happening to my tits than with my asshole or my dick, and that kind of makes me loose my bead on what's really going on. I hate sounding like a know-it-all but, dammit, this fucking business, and I do mean this fucking business, is like walking on eggs sometimes. If its going to have any success at all you got to go in with the best hand you can get. Both of you.

Or maybe even in the three's sometimes.

Or four!

Five!

Hell, who knows!

Who cares!

For a bunch of us this sex game is pretty much all we've got, so we count on it a lot, but we got to be considerate of one another.

Tolliver was fucking me with an easy tempo now, like he'd got the piece down good. He had and I liked it. Then he suggested—and not using too many words either—that I play with his asshole some more.

Hot dog!

I did that, and gladly, because, among other things, I like the feel of an asshole, the idea of it, sexually speaking. Like it's something you've found hidden someplace that you aren't really supposed to have, something that belongs to someone else except that it's yours just for right now.

And so I stroked and smoothed Tolliver's asshole, and doing it I imagined it making those twitchy puckers, those tight, screwed-up little grins that they do.

I rubbed it while I was thinking about laying kisses on it.

And more than that, I thought about the licks and kisses and sucks I could and should lay on it because tomorrow I might not have anything like this at all. And so, guided by perversity and with just a little nudge, I pushed one finger through the hole. I felt the usual wickedness in knowing that what I'm doing—all this stuff—isn't the intended way. Oh but that's nothing new, not at all, because I've felt wicked all my life, ever since I knew what wicked was. You get used to it.

So I goosed the guy's asshole again, and he came down on my mouth in a real pressing search for kisses, but it went on to a lot more than that. In a mess of hot spit we sucked our tongues twisted in a snake-fuck coil as if in their silent contortions was held the keys to the locks we wanted so badly to smash open. More than once sharp teeth came a little beyond the grin, not brutal though, but with bite enough to unsettle the complacent ignorance of pain, and that heightened the disorderly thrill in the perception of the various concerns spinning along toward the time when only that one thing would matter—when getting your rocks off was the only thing that mattered.

Hugged down close he was pumping his dick as if he thought I might turn into stone any minute and he'd better hurry up. His mouth was moving all over my throat and face laying down a track of kisses and bites, the bites, as I said, not always being on the gentle side. Well, when I shoved two fingers up his asshole, Tolliver straightened up on me like his name had been called out by somebody important. Oh my, for a second or two everything damn near shut down, and then I jammed my fingers again. And, oh shit, that did it. He started laying into me with a fierce bundle of jabs that, if I was ever to believe any of that crap, surely came from Lucifer's own little set of tortures. Jesus, but the guy let loose. And I caught on to it too. I could feel the thumping and pumping in my guts and I knew that pretty fucking quick I'd be shooting for the stars. I grabbed hold of Tolliver's butt cheeks to pull him on, and shit, in just a few more stabs, I was put on the list of goners.

Oh Lord Jesus Christ, man, all of a sudden there was jizz shooting all over the place.

Mine.

Healthy spurts too. Hot.

Then Tolliver hollered, and loud too, "I'm gonna come, man! I'm fuckin' gonna fuckin' come!"

He's about to come! he hollers, and there, goddammit, *I* was creaming a whole fucking wad on my belly and chest, and while *my* asshole was still turning the crank on *his* dick. Oh, goddammit, I was in the sick hell of heaven and loving it, and he was still talking about it! Then, punching at my asshole like it was a favorite toy, he laid more hard kisses on my mouth. All I could do was let him go and hold my breath while the horses I thought I owned dragged me off down the fucking road.

Oh boy.

"I'm gonna come, Scotch!" he hollered out again, saying my name for the first time.

"Okay," I said, "come! Come!"

"Oh shit, I'm gonna come!"

133

I tightened up all my screws and nuts so's to be ready to give him a good toss when it come down to the second, and God, when it did hit it hit like a high wind behind a lumber truck. Smash! The guy went to pieces like I never seen anyone do before. He shivered and quaked and jerked, and all the while moaning under his breath like he was trying to tell a secret to a long dead relative. Where most of the time all that ruckus from start to finish is over in just a matter of ten, fifteen seconds, this guy was strung out on it for a long time. Which was all right though. Yeah, all right! The thing was, he was pulling me along like dead weight. Not dead like I wasn't up to participating. No, I was doing that plenty. I just didn't know where the hell we were going. He was pounding me and moaning and carrying on like there might be some secret pervert he was trying to impress watching from behind the teevee. There wasn't, of course, so I just lay there to take the news as he delivered it. And doing it, he sure as hell did us both a big favor. God! Though I'd already shot my wad, he whacked me out like I thought I'd never come again. Lord!

In a little bit all that simmered down, like it always does of course, and pretty soon Tolliver rolled off me and onto the floor. He lay there with his face against the rug really still for quite a while. I hoped he wasn't suddenly sick. He was too young and healthy looking for having a heart attack.

Pretty soon though he came up on his elbows.

"Jesus Christ," he said, "that was one helluva fuck."

Still feeling giddy and not being a clod, I said, "Thank you."

Then he asked, "Is there anything to drink around here? Any booze?"

"No, there isn't anything to drink around here."

"Oh damn," he muttered and shook his head like he was faintly disgusted.

"Sorry," I said.

But I didn't really mean it.

So we made some small talk, and pretty soon there was enough of that so we started getting dressed. Before I got my pants pulled up Tolliver bent down and kissed my dick. He smiled and said next time maybe he wouldn't be so horny and then he'd take better care of that. I don't know. I guess we'll just have to wait and see because he was all buttoned up, smoothed down, and gone in another three minutes or so.

So there was another one down, but I'm not making any complaint.

Since I'm no longer in Pea Ridge I haven't got one thing to complain about. Nossir. When the time come for me to finally get out of there, when things were finished up as good as they could be—the funerals and all is what I'm referring to—about the youngest person left, not counting the no-account itinerants, was Mr. Prendom, the druggist, and he was at least fifty. Captive old people and trashy vagabonds was about all that was left, and not a whole lot in the way of a future for anyone. Oh Jesus, nobody ever could get me to go back to that place.

So, since I come over here I've done all right. It hasn't been too easy finding work of course. I worked at Hominy Bob's for almost six months. I didn't like it but it was okay except for that fucking Nick. He was a part owner, that was true, but, Jesus Christ, he still didn't have any kingly right to be trying to make a guy all the fucking time. It gets tiresome having to find diplomatic ways to say to a guy to buzz off. Of course, in all honesty, if he'd had some hair and wasn't so fat there might have had some chance. But, then again, probably not. He was a shitass and nothing could change that, neither hair nor anything else. I'd just come out of the hills, that was true, and I'm not too well educated, that's also true, but I do have some integrity and I've erected standards of sorts. Simply put, I do not go with anybody who doesn't turn me on in some way. It's just too damned hard getting excited. Now I admit there's a lot of ways to get turned on to a guy, and a little money here and there won't hurt things much, but I don't think it's a good idea to get that kind of widespread reputation. There's some guys around who don't care. But I do.

I know quite a lot of guys from a few bars and other places that I hang out at. I don't do much drinking, looking back on what it did to my dad and his dad—and a couple of cousins too—but I don't come down heavy on others if they choose to do it just as long as I'm not pulled in.

Like this guy I met maybe three weeks ago at a place called Laredo, over by the packing houses.

Somewhere around I suppose forty, he was good-looking, top of the line dresser and all that, but he had a snoot full, almost staggering. He sent me two beers by way of the bartender and being that three's my limit I was going to leave. I stopped on the way out to say thanks.

He wanted to get me another.

I held up my hand.

135

"No," I said, "no more today. I got to go."

"No more?"

"No."

"Well, will you tell your name then?"

"Scotch."

"Really?"

"Really."

"Well, how about that."

Up close, though reddened and loosened from the booze, he was more attractive than I'd thought. And he looked somehow caught out, maybe lost or confused or something. Out of his element. Anyhow, he didn't look like he was where he should be or really wanted to be. In some vague way I wished he wasn't drunk, and at the same time I wished I wasn't standing there talking to him either. He told me his name was Dan. After a little more awkward talk it was decided we'd go out and get some coffee and maybe something to eat.

We went down the street to Sandy's Burger Barn.

Away from the bar and a little ways on the road to sobering up he was turning more and more into a pretty nice fellow, in a hesitant, shy sort of way.

Booze wasn't his friend at all.

Well, we ate some burgers and fries, and talked for about an hour. Then I walked with him the couple of blocks to his car. He said he was okay to drive now and did I want to go somewhere else.

"Not right now," I said.

"I won't make you uncomfortable," he said.

"I'm just going home," I said. "I can walk. It isn't far."

Dan shrugged slightly and looked off down the street.

Then, his voice low and husky, he said he'd like to see me again.

"Would that be okay, Scotch?" he said.

"Yeah. I guess that'd be okay," I said.

"When?"

"Oh," I said, deciding to go for a simple shot, "you could find me here on this corner tomorrow afternoon."

It was Eighth and Tucker.

"Okay. What time?"

"About six."

"Okay."

I waved and walked away. His car was new and not cheap. A snazzy foreign make, I'm sure. It was a bright, bright red, almost orange. Very shiny and very rich looking.

That next day I didn't really expect the guy to show up because people drinking aren't your most reliable types, but he did and looking a *whole* lot better without the strings of booze pulling him down. And he was standing on the sidewalk, not sitting there in his car like a stakeout. That made a good impression on me.

"Hi, Dan," I said.

"Hello, Scotch."

We shook hands.

Dan smiled sort of nervously.

"I'm really glad you came, Scotch," he said. "I was afraid maybe you'd think I was all hot air. Alcohol sometimes talks too much. Most of the time as a matter of fact."

I nodded but didn't say nothing. There wasn't much point in laboring the obvious.

Not as tall as me, he had that careful look about him that you see in men who are aware of the passing by of time and have enough money and objective to do something about it. One... well, two of those things being to have some nice clothes and a nice car.

Man, that's a good start... for anything!

Dan asked if I wanted to sit in the car.

"Yeah," I said, "that'd be okay."

And it was nice in there. The leather squeaked when you moved on it, and there were enough dials and buttons strung around to occupy some kind of technician. The stereo was low but still had a good sound, making me think of the kind of movie—perfect and untrue—where the shit that ordinarily hangs on almost everything can't be seen. I felt good but cautious. Dan was sitting in a sideways position, a leg pulled up, and I could see under his not tight slacks that he was more than likely pretty big. And that, I knew, could put us on the right track right off if a few other things panned out okay.

I waited a little bit to give him time to say something.

"Well, what do you think, Scotch?" he said.

"What do I think?" I replied, being kind of coy which is something I really hate.

"Well, like what kind of a chance do I stand with you now that I'm sober?"

I thought, well, the guy is fucking direct, and there sure isn't anything wrong with that.

"I don't see any problem right off, Dan," I said. "I'm not totally against booze. Nothing personal here, but I just don't mix a lot with it or with those who do."

"I can understand that easy enough."

Like I do a lot of the time, I flashed for a decision right then and it flashed yes. Then I usually just let events follow. This time, though, I looked Dan square in the face, my intent being to force along some of those events by offering open, frank interest. I know, it's sort of cheap, but it works.

"I take that as a yes," he said.

I nodded.

Then he smiled and said, "Okay, young man, now I'll put you on the spot. When?"

"What's wrong with now?"

"You bet."

He started the car.

"I'm at a motel," he said. "Is that okay?"

"Sure, that's okay."

Well, I've been to my share of motels since I come over here. Yeah. Sometimes it ended up being overnight and sometimes, well, most, for just an hour or two. And some occasions have been more successful than others, but it always seems to be with the older, more careful type guys that I mentioned before.

It doesn't matter, of course. It's just the fall of things, I guess.

But the motel in this case was in the better category of the class. Legitimate. By that I mean like it wasn't just someplace—some flop—he'd gotten just in case he landed himself a toss. It had a covered garage instead of the drive up parking place, and there was a covered walkway around to all the doors so's to give it a more permanent appearance. Anyhow, it was okay, and hell, it wasn't even my choice to make in the first place.

We went right in, and so's to keep things moving, as I was giving the place the once-over I was pulling my shirt out of my pants just like I'd do stripping down at home. By the time I'd checked out the plastic furniture and the big orange flowers on the bedspread I was without shirt and tee. I popped open my pants which showed the white bunchiness of my boxer underwear, which is always sexy to me since I saw a hunky guy do it in a movie. Pushing off my boots, my pants went down to my thighs, and I looked at Dan sort of sideways as if to say, well, c'mon, fella. Hell, it works a lot better than hot snot. He looked like somebody'd just given him free tickets to all the highest and fastest rides at the new carnival show just rolled into town.

"Jesus Christ," he muttered, and started stripping off his clothes.

I took in his muscular legs—those of an athlete—and the neat torso, and felt good that I hadn't made a mistake.

After he was naked, which wasn't long, I guided him back to a chair by the bed. His dick, up to hard play in nothing flat, was one of the neat kind. The head was long and sleek and sort of rounded like a giant pecan. Wherever you might decide to put it you knew it was going to go in meaning strictly business. I stood there letting him get a good look at mine—which always makes me think of a torpedo—and then I went down on my knees to give him a let's-work-up-to-it suck. You know, the guy was at a twitch almost right from the start, and that put me in the frame of mind that he might be a one shot fella. That wasn't bad, but I wanted more because I liked him, liked his carefully cultured body, his sleek dick, and the way he didn't just bang right in taking everything for granted.

After sucking a while and doing a lot of work with my tongue around the head, I came up.

"Do you like coming more than once?" I said.

"Well, yes," he replied slowly as if any idea of how things might go was just forming in his head. Then: "Why, sure!"

I figured from that that he was probably telling the truth because he still had this look that said he'd just come to the party, was still sorting things out. You know how some guys, after they come and no matter what they say before, want to scram just as soon as they can. That's always a sort of let down, like you've been used as a piece of convenient plumbing.

139

Anyway...

"Good," I said. "Do you think you'd like fucking me?"

His pretty blue eyes got real big.

"Oh hell yes," he said.

I decided to move right along. No need calling the shots on that kind of enthusiasm.

I got my little tube from my pants and started greasing us up, doing it fast because to me its kind of like peeling potatoes, but it's something you got to do for a smooth performance. He went for it big though, smiling for all shitty hell. He would've gone big for anything in his horny condition, but that was all right because it made me feel even more handy at doing that ole deed once again.

Sort of backing up, I took him in while he was still sitting in the chair, a raunchy, frenchy, fuck-the-neighbors beginning. But, as you probably know, it doesn't do for the long haul. I swung my butt a little in a whorish way to further open up the session, feeling the dick in me like the offering of some noble, city-living gent who comes around only once or twice a year about the time the crops are in. The fit was good and the feel of the whole stroke seemed a definite go.

"I'm going to go down on the floor now," I said over my shoulder. "You come with me and don't let your dick slip out if you can."

"Okay."

"And then when we're down there you can do whatever you want. Do whatever you want. Okay?"

"Okay."

"I mean it now."

He grinned.

Well, he did it like he was born to it—neat—setting right into a rolling screw, slapping his hips against my butt as if he took it from some sudden idea in his head that he had all this coming to him. That was all right. I didn't have to teach him, urge him, lead him, show him how to do anything. I was down and he was up, just the way I like it to be, well, for the time being anyway.

"Now do just whatever you want," I reminded him, wishing I could see his handsome, charge-card face.

"If I do much more right now," he said, "I'm going to come."

I considered that.

"Well," I said, "go ahead and come if you want. That's okay. We can do some more later on."

As we screwed, bumping and humping along, I wondered when this desirable man last has his dick in any kind of hole, and was glad, oh so glad, it was mine that his rod was prodding now. I had my hand on my own, savoring its hard I'm-alive-and-this-is-my-dick feeling when there was a stiffening in me, a new rigidness above me.

Oh ho ho! There was a change a-coming down.

"Oh shit!" Dan cried. "Oh holy shit!"

"You coming?"

"Yeah. Oh God!"

The play wasn't all that long but the ending was just as good as any I could expect because the guy was so excited, so energetic, in going right to the root of the matter. He needed and wanted to be fucking a butt and he *was* fucking a butt and now he was going to pop a wad while doing it. You can't beat that. And I was glad it was my butt being of service. And the coming part was just as neat. He quivered and pitched and rolled and turned, trying through it all, it seemed, to get even farther into me. I shugged back at him to take all the paste he had to give. Soon enough, after making a few more contortions, he slumped down, a laid out heap on my back, slick, spent, and had. He kissed and licked me behind an ear while his hands cruised my belly between my tits and cock.

"Oh Jesus, Scotch," he whispered. "It's been so damned long..."

"I know, man."

And the not-so-funny truth was that I probably did, not so much the fact but the essence of it. But there really wasn't much of anything to be had in talking about it.

"Did you come?" he asked.

"No."

"Oh shit."

"But I will later."

"Okay. And that's a promise?"

"Yeah."

Maybe fifteen minutes later we were back at it in what ended up being, and right up to the snapping of the ribbon, a classic sixty-nine. It started out with him looking me over from head to foot like he wanted to be really sure of what he had. I'm sure it wasn't his intention, but I was inspected like a used car, but it was kind of fun wondering where he'd go off to next. Soon enough he was kissing and licking me in all the important places and, just as soon as a toad can zap that firefly, I was up and ready. He was over me with my legs up and behind his arms so's to get a good go at the licking of my asshole. His dick was right there above my face strung out with its nifty head looking around for someplace to go. I did the natural thing and put my mouth on it, and he followed the play. We settled down into that clever position, probably made up by some ancient guys before they could even talk about it, and went on about the pleasure of mutual cocksucking. I didn't know why and wasn't going to ask—and really *couldn't* right then anyhow—but he seemed awful fucking good at all this for a guy who was represented as being in a kind of deprived situation. For one thing he could go down on it the whole length without any great toil and stay down there long enough for it to do some good. About the fifth time he did it I could feel the little sizzle around the head of my dick and I knew that he was going to be having me thataway whether he knew it or not. Meantime, of course, I was tending to him by making my every effort mount up to a heap high enough to make him willing and able to jump off again. Willing didn't seem to be a problem, and able—that dick wasn't bashful about poking down my throat—was just a matter of time. So I licked and sucked his balls and the other neat folds in the same area, even going far enough to take a quick peek at his asshole—pretty, pink, and tight—although I was saving that for a little something a little later on. It seems that if you stay with one fella long enough to get past the pressing demands of the immediate needs, sometimes the trips that follow can be longer and maybe even deeper—no joke intended, folks— if there isn't that compelling urge to get up right away and run off. And then before you know it, you have to start thinking about finding yourself another guy. I know what I'm talking about because, dammit, I do it myself!

So there I am down there with my head between this guy's legs doing my Pea Ridge best to render an uptown style blowjob while the Hottentot bells are starting to ring in my balls. And then, dammit, he jerked away from me in a sort of reflexive way before shoving forward again real fast, going deep into my throat. That was followed by some side to side rolls like something was out of control. He was by the fuck of God going to come!

Again!

Already!

I was thrilled, of course, but not prepared. No matter, because in just a few seconds here it come barreling out of his dick into my mouth in mighty squirts attended by a whole choir of singers, all with different ideas on how to sing that haphazard song. In that sprawling confusion with all the random seizures going on, my gang just had to get in on the act and, Jesus, it was one hell of a showdown, a real Saturday night hayride! I started shooting into his mouth, jamming my hips against his face, feeling that I'm-going-to-die rush as his tongue wrapped around the head of my dick welcoming out the fat, clumsy drops. I closed my knees over his ears, waiting for an eternity before going into the wilt that's to be found in that slovenly peace. Oh Lord, when two guys get their arrangements together there isn't anything else that packs that same knock-your-socks-off wallop. No siree! Nothing! It's like having a special gift from some fat god who has nothing to do but sit around on his can and hand out those hot ejaculations.

"A what?" I said. I couldn't hear his words because he was still nosing around in my butt.

"A harlot," he said louder, coming up and looking me square in the face. "I said a har... "

"Yeah, I heard. Maybe you'd care to elaborate on that?"

"Well... no. But I wouldn't mind the description myself."

"No? Good, because you got it."

"Really? Me?"

"Yeah, you. You just as much as anybody else."

"Well, how marvelous!"

How marvelous he says. Marvelous!

Now, how do you like that?

The guy is just burning up with enthusiasm to be called a whore. Of course, I've always known in the back of my mind and at the bottom of my heart that that applies to me and always has.

Oh hell, I've always been a slut. Even before I first messed around with my cousins at about age seven, and probably even before that except I didn't have the beans to put any of it together. But now that time has

143

hardened me off and the high-pitched exhortations of the slicked down backwoods preachers in saddle shoes ring in my ears no more, all those words, the whole damned dictionary of them so rich in texture and impression, come now in comforting enlightenment because they describe me in the terms of the world how I am and how that acceptance abides in me in comfort. Fuck man, it's old, it's simple, and it's difficult, but once you accept who you are and on your own terms nobody can hurt you no matter what the hell they say.

Or think.

You bet.

So I said to Dan, "You know, you got a nice ass. A harlot's ass."

"You think so?"

"Yeah, and I got me some hot designs on it."

"Really!"

"Yeah!"

"When?"

"Right now."

He was lying on his stomach diagonally across the bed. Going up on my knees, I gave his foxy butt a couple of playful slaps, and then fell down, hugging and roughhousing him, getting my legs wound in with his and him in a nelson hold. I suppose it goes back to the days of stone clubs and naked bodies but there sure is a sexiness in forcing another man, even harmlessly and playfully, into a submissive position. Right then, without going any farther than that, I was getting a roaring hard-on. But there was an even more squalid impulse crouched in me, hairy and dark and peering out behind shrouded eyes. I wanted, in a whirl of evilness, to do something to really hurt this man, to mark him and watch him be hurt. Holding him in the nelson, all the ruthless things I could do started tumbling through my head, and I know if I *had* had a club I'd probably have smashed it on his head and did what I wanted to do—all of it—every hair raising, swollen-tongued perversion I could think of. Horrified in small attacks, I slammed all that away fast, locked it down tight. I would have, if I could have, denied it but I couldn't. Sports, politics, and war must find their big popularity on account of that bag of shit. And so, instead of doing anything homicidal, I started delivering kisses to the back of his neck. The effect was just as good, minus the blood and, later of course, the guilt and the punishment, and that's to say nothing about the burden of remorse.

Well, the Vaseline was handy so I slapped that on real fast and pulled him to me.

"Okay, baby," I said softly, "here we go."

"Go easy, Scotch. It's been a long time."

That, I have to say, turned me on even more. I mean, a virgin might have been out of the question but someone who's been lying fallow for a while—how long?—wasn't. With his legs pushed apart, my knees together, I went in. I don't know what it is—well, I do—but when that little doohickey of human flesh opens up, pushes apart to accept me—my cock, my me—I am lifted up high to a kind of joy, yeah, a damned joy that goes way, way past what really amounts to no more than putting your dick into an unintended hole. In some sense I suppose lust and prayer—more than prayer, supplication—spring from the same vein because they both carry hope.

So that's sort of what I felt going into this guy's asshole, that tattered little refugee, hope.

Of course, like I say, I don't know how long he'd been without but there weren't any hesitant hitches in the penetration. The thing reached its warm mark gliding in with the grandeur of an ancient, but friendly, creature come up from deep water. Pressed close to him, my hands clamped to his nice shoulders, I ventured out on stroll across wide lawns where trees, some still young, grew in handsome groves, all of them full with leaves. Knowing that hidden from the sight of all creation, my dick was contacting his body and his guts in a way that was kind of terrible and yet happening—as if it was ordained—I was once again nailed by a screwball feeling of hope.

I pushed my hand under his belly to find his dick and hold it. It was hard but not hasty in demand, lying there warm in the basket of this screwing.

"God, Scotch" Dan murmured, "I'd forgotten what this could be like."

Hearing those words made me feel like I was doing so much more than just dealing out another comfy ride.

"How long's it been?" I asked, experiencing a need to know that I just couldn't squelch.

"Oh hell. Years."

"Years?"

145

"Years, Scotch."

"How come?"

"It's a long story. Maybe later, okay?"

That was good enough. That was all I needed to know, and I didn't know why the hell I needed to know *that*.

"You want to turn over?" I said.

I didn't want to say it right out but I wanted to look into his eyes. I was doing something I'd been doing for years, and yet here it was in some way somehow new. Now, is that possible?

"Okay," he said.

During that tricky move, when he was in a sort of little boy position with his legs drawn up, he looked up at me and smiled in a waywardly innocent way.

"I bet you do this a lot, don't you?" he said.

"Well, yes," I replied. "Yes."

I looked at him trying to appear casual.

"Why do you ask?" I said.

"No reason," he said. "I was just interested."

Goddammit! I blushed in hot waves while moving his legs up on my shoulders, and I didn't even want to consider why.

Putting the head of my dick against his asshole and poised to go back in, I was so excited I was sure I would pop my nuts right there without any real kind of provocation. I felt, dammit! a urgent need to explain myself, to try and share the meaning I found in this meaty business we were about to start up yet once again. Just as I was going in, just as I was doing something I knew something about, our eyes met and he flashed me another of those innocent smiles full of more sexual—and, hell, I guess even more than that—significance than I'd ever received before. And, of course, I flooded with another blush. I had just what I'd wanted, which was to be looking into his eyes, and now that I had it, I was fucking embarrassed.

Well, shit!

So, I started the trek feeling like this was the first time I'd ever undertaken such a mission. Can you imagine that! Lucky for me, my youthful ardor—meaning by that the hard-on—didn't suffer under the affliction of that embarrassment. If anything the whole rigmarole was being stoked up to a higher plane by this confusion and delicate uncertainty.

Then, oh by Christ, reaching up and putting his arms around my neck he pulled me down for a real long kiss.

"You're right," Dan said after planting that one. "This position is much nicer. Let's go!"

Let's go! Whoa! Are we supposed to be going to a horse race with this talk of lets go! Are we involved in some sort of competition here that I don't know about? Huh? No, of course not. And so, not one to hang back under any erotic circumstances, in just a few seconds I had everything pretty well under control again. My equilibrium reestablished, we got on with the business at hand which was calling up butt fucking's ole velvety spell.

I suppose if it wasn't for the basic simplicity of the sex game itself there wouldn't be much enthusiasm for it at all. What I mean is, with the aim being so obvious, it's in the trying to get transported there that gives rise to all the challenges, and who would want to participate in it at all if it was any more complicated that it already is, even being as simple as it is.

But we, Dan and me, we climbed in that very personal way up to the plateau and, even though the view from up there was nice, the demands being made by this fuss growing up between us in the genital area wouldn't allow for anything but devotion to its urgency. Having overcome that twinkling little bit of embarrassment earlier, I was now delving deep into his eyes, as well as his butt, seeking what almost everybody seeks without ever being ready to give it a name. Anyhow, I was buried in his ingenuous eyes, springing with liquid ease from them to the invitation to kiss. Our first exertion lay in the headway being made in concert between his asshole and my dick, and that exertion was working fast up to that one very short, very hot moment. Dan's asshole was now deep to the stroke and I felt in every new lunge that I was being given something that I had no right to have.

"Scotch," Dan whispered, "if I blow my nuts I'm afraid I'll have to stop."

"Are you about to?"

"Not yet."

"Tell me when."

I slowed the action way down. "If you want to stop, just tell me."

"No, I don't want that. You come when and how you want."

That sounded pretty familiar to me and, knowing who said it, I made

147

some hot, wet plans. "You come, sweetheart, and ole Scotch'll be right behind a-holding you up."

I meant what I said, and I had a good firm conviction that I could back it up. By that I'm saying that my dick, and the package of plumbing that makes it all work, had gone to capacity operation and, with just a few well-timed pushes, we would be up and over and into the promised land in no time at all. So, keeping the program in mind, I made the triple assault against the fella by jacking him off, kissing him, and fucking him, and pretty soon I could feel the whole effort gathering up the juice to blast off the top of the mountain one more time. Keeping my strokes even and steady I flattened out the kisses into some really fast licks and sucks, mindless but direct in their intent. Jesus, in a such a goddamned drench of passion I didn't think much of anything could last very long, and it didn't.

"Oh, Scotch!"

I knew what it was, of course.

I started the final pump required of me, and when that first zing jolted from my asshole into my dick, I moved back, and with the pleasant disposition of a monarch observing the populace at play, I watched what we had wrought. My dear, I let 'er rip and dropped a load into the guy with hot squirts that I were somehow more than the product of the pelvic quiver.

"Oh, Scotch! Shit! Shit! Shit!"

Dan was now at the not always tender mercies of his body in its constant struggle for a future. Whatever its capacity as the mastermind of the operation, the brain and all the dignitaries seated therein are constantly badgered for attention by the rascals and crybabies who are responsible in one way or another for keeping the show on the road. And right now it was the sexual imps who had run of the place. So there Dan was, twisting under this big load of neat-o stress brought to him by that hellish trinity crowned Peter, Asshole and Mouth. In a more or less helpless situation he was being slapped around several times over by that selfish crew. With all that potent magic hitting him at once, his patient good looks had taken on a hunted raggedness in which his eyes caught mine as if seeking some kind of reassurance. I had given him all I could right then. It was all pretty much a done deal now: the jizz had been splashed and splattered about in yet another repleted onanism. His dick was still preening in a sick-pretty strain and his belly was sending out the word that the dance, though hot, would be

148

shutting down before long now. I was still keeping a beat myself to run up the tally to a high figure but I could see on Dan's face that we had bought enough. I pulled out and bent down to kiss him, feeling that he earned a congratulation of some sort. He received the kiss through short, wet gasps.

"Honest to Christ," he said, still giddy with relief even after a period of recovery, "we're just a couple of sex-crazy fools!"

His enthusiasm was new, clear, unblemished, and, yeah, dammit, fine. Yeah fine.

"You bet," I agreed, "two fucking fools all right."

I moved down to lay along side the other fool and he, maybe still feeling the emotional stroke of coming down from the high place, put his hand on my chest and bestowed on me a few of the deepest kisses—not born of a despotic passion—I'd had in a long time. So soon after the clatter and clang of the other, the feeling conveyed in those and the caresses that escorted them was laden with a tenderness that was almost shocking in its substance. Then, with a smile almost painful to receive, he gazed at me in a pensive way as if trying to sort flower petals from bee's wings. I felt the gently grinding edges of fraudulence put in as they sometimes do when I come upon the traces of an artless innocence.

"We couldn't do this if I was drunk," Dad said.

"No."

He sighed.

"Would you have even tried?"

"No."

"Well, I can understand that."

Dan kissed me again. The tenderness was still there but also present was a current of resolve, or of some kind of optimism, rolled in with a wise awareness of fact. He tweaked my dick and then swung around to the edge of the bed.

"Shower with me?" he said.

"I'll rest a bit. I'll go after you."

"Okay. Then how about some steak and eggs? Isn't that the usual, you know, man stuff?"

"Yeah, I guess it is."

The shower noise and the rumpled bed, with me still in it, seemed at first a comfortable bounty in its assumed familiarity. Stretching, I surveyed

149

the casually intimate scene. Then like a bolt, the scattered clothes and remnants of fuck—the pursuit of it!—suddenly bore up the shocks of a disquieting expectation. Following hot on all that was a broadcast burst of disquieting visions dealing mainly with me and my indefinite future that were so exhausting in their trampling confusion that I felt sickly and tired. I was overwhelmed with something much too close to revulsion for everything I could see to allow for any further lassitude. Scrambling from the bed I began dressing in a hurried, mindless haste as if expecting an impending chase by all the crime-stoppers of modern myth, Elliot Ness included. God, I was building guilts I hadn't even properly surveyed yet! The exit from the room was itself blooming with cowardice: I pulled the door closed with the knob turned to avoid that telltale click. And then at a stiffly brisk pace, much to panicky to run, I fled that motel keeping, for the life of me, to the side streets until I was easily eight blocks away. Then, squaring my shoulders in pretending what I had done I had not, I went on to my own not so spiffy pad.

Bread, pickles, and pork 'n' beans have been in my, uh, nutritional program since I was a whelp in Pea Ridge, and that's what I ate late that night. I hated every bite for reminding me of, yeah, Pea Ridge—and why, being here, I wasn't doing a whole lot better than I would be if I was there. I was, as never before in my life, beset by a fuckingly profound feeling of discontent and failure. And all because some guy, nice and kind of sweet, though more than a little older than me and who, more than likely, was saddled with a drinking problem had fucked me and wanted to take me out to get something to eat. Well, my God, is that what's bothering you, buddy? Wake up and, as they say, smell the coffee, bluebird. This may not be two steps down from heaven but it also sure isn't the space two steps up from hell you'd occupied by Pea Ridge, Kentucky neither. So, wrapped up then in the bandages of quiet acceptance—I'm pretty good at it—I watched my Salvation Army teevee for a while, then showered and went to bed. In the dark I thought a little more about Dan, and what it was or why it was that I had to run away like that. If I did know the reason it wasn't lying near the surface and I wasn't in the frame of mind to do much digging for it. I had learned in the scratchy days of boyhood in the shadows of a drunken father and a battered mother, not to scrutinize too closely what you have, and don't, even if it's really rotten, expect it to get much better either. Thataway there isn't much room for disappointment. It was a stoicism instilled those years ago along with an uncomplaining acceptance of the righteousness of bread, pickles, and pork 'n' beans.

And so it goes.

Two days later while making the rounds I landed a job at a pretty decent restaurant—Alice's Cozy Pantry—busing dishes and doing the usual general kitchen duties. It's not at all bad for what it is and the food's pretty good, too—a lot better selection than chilidogs, fries, and coke. They have things like pretty salads, fresh vegetables, and specials that change every day. And, the Lord be, there's bread baked fresh every day right there.

Yeah, Alice's Cozy Pantry is nice and even kind of classy.

When I was working and it was slow between meals I thought about Dan sometimes, and about of going maybe to Laredo to see if he'd be there but, dammit, I'd get embarrassed just thinking about it. I mean, what the hell would I say and all that. Especially after running out like I did. How could I begin to explain the feeling of just being overcome by the possibility that something might happen between us, and I, the hotshot two-stepper, couldn't handle it.

Jesus goddamn!

Sometimes it tough thinking through that kind of a confusion.

Then just the other night I saw Tommy as I was passing Hominy Bob's and he hailed me to come on in. Tommy's okay if you keep an arm's length from him because I've heard some tough stuff told about him. Like being into drugs, hot merchandise, stolen cars now and then, and procurement. He's a good-looking guy and kind of imposing when you're looking on as any kind of an aspirant. That's okay. All I ever wanted to do was make it with him, and I did that.

"Hey, bub, I ain't seen ya for awhile," he said.

"Maybe a couple of weeks."

"Yeah, 'bout that."

"Yeah."

He smiled, his teeth incredibly white and even.

"Say," he said, "I got this score coming up later if ya want in on some hot action."

"What kind of score?"

"Oh, some friends got theirselves a new boy. Gonna break him in.

151

Interested?"

"Maybe."

"Need maybe a dozen. Done got eleven including me. You makes the twelve."

I looked intently at this fella. He was as close to organized crime as I would ever be likely to get, and I sure didn't want to come off being any kind of rube, being as we were both active on the street.

"How old's the boy?" I asked.

"Sixteen, seventeen. Maybe fifteen."

Oh my!

"He's a good-lookin' little number too," Tommy said. "It's gonna be one hot fuckin' deal, man."

There floated through me a barge bigger than a football field loaded with all the trappings of dissolution I could possibly imagine: naked clowns fucking dogs, lines of priests of all manner of faith happily drunk and dancing The Madison, earthbound cocks sending heavenward comets of jizz. You know, that sort of thing. I was excited. The traversal of that barge was accompanied by brassy and very loud music of the giddiest kind.

"Yeah. Sure," I said, worldly and suave. "I think I could go for that."

"Gonna cost ya, bub. He's gonna be sweet."

"Yeah? How much?"

"Fifty."

Well, the man of sophistication, the man known to be of worldly pursuits, had to swallow hard in a way unobserved.

Fifty bucks!

Jesus Christ, I thought, that's a whole week's rent!

"Yeah," I said. "Good deal. Go ahead and put me down for it."

Tommy sighed.

"The money's gotta be paid up front, sport," he said. "This ain't but a one time deal and there ain't no credit to be had."

"Oh. Yeah," I said and paid out the fifty thinking, oh God, it's going to be pork 'n' beans for a month.

Tommy had an address and a date printed out neatly on small pieces of blue paper, like invitations to an annual event of some prestige.

I got one.

Oh boy!

Right then I figured it was well worth all those beans and pickles.

"Now this is for one guy only," Tommy said. "Don't try to bring nobody else or you won't get in. And don't bring no booze. Grass is okay. But no booze, okay?"

"No booze," I repeated.

The deal set up, I set out for the second half of a split shift at Alice's Cozy Pantry hoping for some decent tips and looking forward to my last good meal for a spell. It was Friday. I wouldn't be working again until Monday. The doings was on Saturday night.

Well, the place appointed for this assignation turned out to be an upholstery shop down in the southeast part of town. I walked there, and even though I'd set out fairly early I still didn't get there until a little after two a.m. which was the appointed starting time. At the front door a scribbled note directed you to go around to the rear and, once there, you had to make your way through several trucks, some cars, and a couple of motorcycles to get to a metal door stuck away behind tall stacks of wooden drums. If it wasn't trashy it was pretty close to it. I knocked. The door opened, I handed Tommy my paper and I was in!

I was a chosen one at the chosen rites!

Oh boy!

Inside, however, there were no milling, frenzied, half-naked celebrants preparing for activities known only to those highly selective in their perversions. There was no brassy music, no piles of burnt meat, no jugs of potent, blinding liquor. Not any of that sort of thing was anywhere in sight. But there were all the things you'd expect to find in just such an upholstery shop. Somehow I was expecting more. I always do.

Well, okay.

Along with probably hundreds of bolts and rolls of fabrics stacked and stuffed in bins and racks—even way up high—there were piles and piles of heathenish-looking polyfoam, cut to sizes and shapes conceived, it seemed, by a demented mind. They looked like inventions without function. An appearance of orderly and possibly maniacal clutter prevailed. Several pieces of furniture, maimed by time and the human anatomy and undergoing restoration, were scattered around. They were now occupied by men all dressed pretty much alike in denim and leather. They chatted quietly. Some nodded to me as I moved toward the back of the room where

153

I figured I could see pretty good.

"I have to caution you, gentlemen." someone said in a raised voice, "that absolutely no smoking is allowed."

"None at all?"

"You heard me. Those wishing to do grass must do it in the john. Thank you for coming and have fun."

Along a short wall, next to a door standing ajar and revealing that john, a table was set with some plastic bowls filled with several kinds of chips and cookies and a nice selection of the big bottles of Cragmont soft drinks. Provided also were a bucket of ice and a stack of Styrofoam cups. The rock music, selected it seemed for the sensibilities of those pushing forty, played over speakers suspended from the ceiling. The mood of the place was composed and hushed, a gathering of established semi-professional men with just the grip of their fingertips on what remained of relative youth.

Seated on an ugly settee, probably new in his great-grandfather's heyday, was a young fella who, yes indeedy, was about fifteen years old, or maybe even younger. Naked but for bulky boxer shorts that hung to his knees, he was decked out in certain accouterments of leather and chrome: a sinewy collar done with gleaming studs, and heavy bands at the wrists and ankles, also with chrome studs. There was a thick belt hanging loosely about his waist. Slender and nubile, he was put together like an intricate, insoluble puzzle, the pieces round and smooth, fetching of the touch like fragrant fruits worn ripe by the hot sun of summer. His legs were pressed together as if he were in a chill. Dark curly hair in Mediterranean abundance tangled softly around his small face that burned now with intense, alert green eyes. He was very pretty. An older guy, done out in leather jacket and chaps without any other street wear, engaged the boy in earnest conversation, a booted foot propped upon the settee, his own backyard exposure as incidental as the wash hung out on a Monday morning.

Soon enough another fellow, dressed in a maroon bathrobe, went up to the settee and joined in the talk for a while. Then they all went around to the back of a big work table where stood a sort of temporary scaffold, slapped together from two by sixes. After the boy had stepped out of the shorts the men ran a chrome chain from an ankle strap up through an eye on the belt to the wrist which was pulled up high on the scaffold. Then it went through an eye up there, on to the two by six and then across to do the same thing coming down. It was really obvious and really quick, for just like that the boy was hoisted up for the festivities. Just by looking at him and thinking about what was going to happen to him brought up the tightening in my underwear. I knew that the other men were being affected the same way because things got very quiet, and when somebody did laugh it sounded forced and much too tinny, much too gay.

"Jim!" someone called, "c'mon and get this thing started."

The guy in the robe, and I'm guessing it was Jim, stood and dropped it off. He had a huge hard-on supported by an effete looking cock ring. From the look of him—his build and demeanor—he was pretty much the boss of what was going on and going to go on there. He was saying something quiet in the boy's ear, and while he was the other guy was slopping big gobs of Crisco on his dick and balls. All this was suggesting that this was not going to be, or expected to be, a gentle job. Then, his dick glistening white in the bluish neon light, Jim squatted down and, pushing into the boy with a knightly arrogance, began fucking him with a commanding presence, making of it the exhibition it was intended to be. The other men—me included—hung back for a little while just watching and quietly feeling themselves and—a restive, edgy bunch—looking around sorting things out. A shuffle step here, a scoot there, and soon we started to cluster closer around the pair going at a fuck as much for our benefit as theirs. Some guys broke out their dicks so's to be jacking off while they watched. There was some touching but it soon became apparent that the idea here was to fuck the suspended boy, sometime and in some sort of order that I didn't yet understand. In maybe six minutes or so, Jim shuddered in a dignified way and was done. He pulled out, smiling stupidly and holding his dick like together they'd just done some kind of worthy deed. Another guy, tall and good-looking—really impressive looking—moved up and started his turn in this captive sodomy by doing some neat thrusts, coming from down low and going high, like he meant to push the kid right up to the ceiling. While I was watching and getting up a lascivious monkey in my pants I felt someone touch my arm. It was Tommy.

He jerked his head toward the scene.

"Jim told me he wants you up for third or four. Get on up there, man. They ain't gonna wait long."

I didn't even know Jim, and so I was very flattered being chosen for anything preferential considering the mercurial scheme of things, at least as I was reading them. We weren't there to sing hymns and, like Tommy said, the mood probably wouldn't be gentlemanly very much longer. So, in the unobtrusive manner demanded by the situation, I made my way to the fore of the group feeling a perverse pride, both in my selection and knowing that not only could I do it but probably to the envy of most of those getting hot watching. Standing there with my dick neat and prepared in my pants, I hyped myself watching the splendid back and butt of the guy sailing in glory ahead of me. I thought it would be just swell to hump into him and thereby upset everything by unleashing an absolute anarchy of an orgy right then, but even the horny hotshot from Pea Ridge knew that that didn't fit well into the protocol of the match as it was expected to unfold. Pretty soon there was some flexing and pumping in the guy, some grunts and a groan with the butt in a clench, and I knew I was going to be up next.

So I stripped down to nothing, and fast.

Jesus, I felt worldly!

Going into the boy just as fast, I thought I should mutter some kind of greeting but changed my mind real quick when the lad sort of keened, as if he was standing on the edge of some private, almost lamentable, passion. He was young and tender, and somehow grievously inadequate for this activity—it perhaps even being forced upon him—and I, in just a flicker of second thought, considered withdrawing and giving it all up. But ole number three, when offered, had certainly elbowed his way right up front to get in on it, hadn't he? Yep. Yessir. And so, dammit, what's wrong? Well... Then, in the perversity of the moment, I remembered that I, at an even earlier age, had started my career, though not trussed, under similar conditions though *not*, of course, with so *many* at once. So I thought, for him—this boy—and from there, and for years into the future, there would be miles and miles of penile thrusts, deeply appreciated, beginning from where I was sticking my dick right now, and that dick, while not lagging, was not really displaying the ambition exemplary in the man chosen for the third slot. The boy was young and tender, yes. Present and willing, also yes I'd say. Hot and heady, yes to that too. The fuck of the future for me here and now? Oh yes! Oh yes! Oh you bet! And so, all those things considered, I set out to deliver the fuck expected of me knowing that whoever this

young fellow was his future deserved the best I could summon up.
Oh boy! What a deal! Huh?

Water cascading down a sheer rock face is a quiet thrill to watch when you're at the bottom looking upward at a power that never ends. The boy's body, suspended like it was, offered the quiet thrill of desire born in sheets of shimmering, falling water. Being made powerless and possessable, established in him was the illusion that each man cherishes as his right of birth: freedom and power. Taking this boy and using him was, like the masked festivals throughout history, a frank and sanctioned deception that, trapped up in time, legitimatized itself. So there in that group—that horny, hot group masked and unmasked—each man present wanted his chance at the boy, to make yet another grab for the power and freedom thought belonging to him alone.

In my precarious strut, in my deliberate flirt with deception, I kissed in homage the asses of legions of deities for allowing me to approach them through the asshole of this comely young man hung up so for just that purpose. His back, in its slender elegance glowing in a gleaming sweat, invited my mastery. His shoulders hiked up in submission bade me seize control. His legs spread in a prepared stance of acceptance gave a foundation for the exquisite butt that harbored and hid his asshole—mine! mine!—of such urgent importance in this rite. Grasping the boy at the hips, I pressed my dick into its hard advantage, each thrust at the beginning crowned with that perfect, tight embrace captured from the rubbery muscle yet a-ripple in defiance. In a bold action—a forceful commitment driving it—I exercised my privilege as the third penetrant by pulling out and, at a conquering stoop, began sweeping kisses and small bites across those heavenly buttocks, moving all the while closer to the fucked center. Then, opening wide the cheeks, I went at the asshole with my mouth, licking and lapping the hole recently used by the excellent dicks in host at this carnal banquet. Jim, at my side and observing, grabbed the idea and bent in front of the boy, taking the waving wand into his mouth. The captive, thus pulled further into the realm of gilded punishment, swung his butt against my face as the course of the engagement widened. Jim now at suck and the lad eager in the pull of it, I lapped the asshole a few more times and then stood. Putting the head on the spot, the shaft ready for the shove, the balls clamoring for the ride, I, perhaps with more than suitable exhibition, put

157

my hands on the boy's shoulders and, with a blatant slowness, entered him once more. The ride in was flawless—the embedding completed with a series of proprietary jabs—and I began once again a measured, quite adult, and perhaps even to say blasé coition. The reach of it was grand, the tenor of the moment was sonorous as my dick did the work expected of it. The liquid and primary thrusts, ancient calls to come into the future, pulled me along a mossy path where laughing breezes poked playfully at my balls and butt, my asshole loose and secure. I could feel the surge of the shot, the old, daringly new shot, finding the grip to come up for another try. In a control learned in the leafy loneliness of Kentucky, I ignored the spinning ball, allowed it to move at its obedient tread until, collected in its witless army, it cast off all nervous pretense and, hell for leather as if it really had a tomorrow, took control and marched out of me and, horns blaring and drums at a beat, into the boy. God! what a fucking deal! I danced in arabesques of shattered light as the hallelujah of life's muddy necessity united us and then cast us apart.

Well, the coins spent, my celebrity having flashed, its moment now sunk in a growing seep of jizz, I pulled out and turned away.

The new candidate was ready, his bid firmly in hand.

After my stellar performance, but not because of it, the mood of the gathering changed from that of somber lust-in-hiding to one of restrained optimism in that the expectations packed in early on now seemed definite possibilities, their realization depending on opportunity, engineering, and, mainly, guts. The boy was taking the fifth or sixth now, I don't know, I'd lost track. In the growing steam a full-blown orgy was finding its dimensions with fellas stripping down, feeling, fucking, sucking, fingering, shooting, dripping, and breathing hard. They were pairing up and peeling off but the center of the attraction, of course, remained on the boy in the scaffold. The men were moving about him, using him and each other in various homosexual ways, but still there prevailed a mood of civility, of restraint, of shared regard in perversion, that was shored up mainly by the self-serving awareness that there was, after all, more than enough of this stuff to go around.

"You gonna take him down?"

"Nah."

"He's already took about eight of 'em."

"He looks all right to me."

"Jesus Christ, up to now he ain't never had it but one at a time."

"He's getting used to it."

"Getting used to it! He's starting to sag!"

"Well, if he starts to bawling, just call me and I'll take him down."

"Okay, he's your brother."

"That's right, man."

I overheard that between Jim and Tommy. Well, life comes in odd slices, and this was probably not the oddest. In a surreptitious admiration I studied Jim for a moment trying to root under that handsome countenance and isolate the quirk that would prompt him to induce—sell, by God?—a brother into this predicament. It was, of course, to no avail because it was so obvious. Then I looked at the boy. Ravaged no doubt and flushed and strained, his face was raised as if in a fatigued entreaty. Even in stress he was prettily angelic, but that quality was given the lie by the now vigorous perversions being mounted against and around him. A fellow, big and burly, had him in an enormous hug as he pounded away, his furry buttocks insistent in the attack. A third man, interested in the thrust, bent low toward the action to garner in the squeeze and crush the aroma of hope—that of jizzy sweat and bodily seepage—that those busy parts perhaps hugely inspired. Others, close in and strung out, gripped and fondled, pushed, squatted, took, delivered, swallowed, choked, and gagged.

"How much, Tommy?"

"About eleven hundred."

"He gets half."

"Jesus, I the fuck know it, Jim! Shit, we'll settle up when these guys're all fucked out and gone home."

"Okay."

"God, you're such a nag sometimes."

Slipping on my shorts I made the short distance to the refreshment table where I decided on creme soda and a handful of onion-flavored barbecue-style corn chips. From the added distance a deeper perspective was visited on the arena at the scaffold, and I saw in it me at my very worst: the shaggy, bowlegged satyr of gossipy fame fully a-drip with the products of his casual lusts. I gasped in commonplace horror, and aspirating as I did on a corn chip there ensued a terrible spate of coughing. Someone, in vigorous form, began pounding on my back. It seemed to help. I swigged some tepid creme soda, and through eyes washed with tears of controlled effort I turned to thank my benefactor. He was a black fella, about my age, peering into my face with genuine concern.

"Thank you," I managed.

"You're welcome." He put a hand on my shoulder. "You gonna be all right?"

"Oh sure."

With his neatly sculpted features—African in plane, American in detail—he could be no other way but extremely handsome, even extending him to the remote recesses of loneliness. His color, that burnished in the fine tropical woods of carved oriental designs, was a warm invitation to touch, to know. And yet he seemed, oddly, more likely an emissary from some multinational corporation to Third World governments rather than a horny thrill-seeker at an early morning fuck party.

Slight, slender—yeah, skinny—he looked like he probably had a set of chrome-plated weights at home. His collectibles were sacked up in very brief briefs, those so becoming on slimmer builds. He gently brushed my back where he had delivered the needed blows.

"You look okay now," he said.

"Yeah, thanks."

He smiled, a ruffle of uncertainty cutting in at the edges of his lips.

He jerked his head toward the milling scene at the scaffold.

"You were first... "

"No, I was third... "

"... when I got here."

"Oh. Sorry. I didn't mean to cut you off like that."

"It's okay."

He touched me on the chest, his eyes first on his fingers and then looking into mine.

"I would like to have been there," he said.

"Strapped?"

"Not necessarily. With you, I mean. Being fucked."

Yeah!

Oh boy!

The place had extensions I hadn't even considered. If there's lots of water, it's the fool who doesn't drink deep.

"Here?" I asked.

"Why not?"

"With people watching?"

"Doesn't bother me."

The train was in the station and the destination clear. The problem resided in figuring out just how to get on the damned thing. So I did the obvious. I shoved my hand into the pouch of my jockey underwear. He followed, coming in more from the side. Then I went into *his* petite pants, both hands now possessing some nice firm buns. That was a good move because with one hand he relegated those briefs to history. His dick, glistening in its colors of night, was erecting itself, bringing up the gifts so tantalizing to kings and queens of old bound in the colder climes northward. I bent to his chest, cleanly muscled in minimum, and spotted a number of kisses there. I licked his tits, going from one to the other.

"I knew I could expect some measure of zeal from you," he said.

His hands, hot and possessive as if conjuring a spell or divining instruction, were filled with my dick and balls. Then a hand went around my waist, pushing between my cheeks, seeking, maybe, the well?

I got rid of the goddamned shorts fast.

Well, my dick did its torrid little dance of release. I don't know if this was the foreboding vision I'd seen earlier, but it seemed harmless enough. I was not embarking on an extended pogrom of maim and pillage with murder at the head of the list and with rape an iron canon of the faith, disembowelment just a joke. So why that awful vision of myself as somehow the nasty progeny of Adolf Hitler and Idi Amin's bound for the sweaty perversions of the twenty-first century? Naked at my side this fellow here, unknown to me in any other way except, for now, as a sexual brother—briskly setting aside any incestuous connotation—was not offering or being offered anything more than a mutual stroking that even in the most luxuriously devious of imaginations could not amount to much more than a hot wad or two delivered into some specified hole in someone's readily, if casually, available body.

Well, forget it.

Oh I'm pretty good at guilt all right, but not that good.

I sat down in a handsome winged chair that was thrown over with a

161

BRIDGES *by Dixon Stalward*

blue sheet dappled with multi-colored paint dribbles—apparently used as a drop cloth—and spread my legs, thrusting up my hips, to get the best play from my dick, which was at its invitational hard best. He, my new slight but not frail friend, backed right up to it, zeroed in on the position and, with just minor adjustments, presto, took it up into anal heaven—zam—with the aplomb you'd expect to find in just such a magician free of Judeo-Christian convenience store hang-ups. In a sedate Victorian glee to match our chair we started the massage, my hands in a friendly grip upon his sizable, very engagingly hard dick. We planted kisses and licks wherever allowed by space and anatomy. It wasn't the position for completion—we knew that— but it was fun for the simple exaggerated denial of the demand for conformity in the 'sex act' as performed in the shadowy little warrens posting satisfaction in the western world.

"Ho ho, that's neat," he said. "Let's move on."

We moved on to a variation on football scrimmage, this reading being obvious to anyone with an imagination given even the slightest prurient kink. We didn't have a football, but we had a dicks and assholes, miles and miles of heart and, dammit all, an inclination to levity, pushing at times close to the goofy which was not in the best furtherance of the agendas gathered there. We were raising a few stately eyebrows. Then we entered the world of ballet, with him at the barre—in this case the work table— doing the studied stances in a mean parody while offering me opportunities for anal penetrations which certain nutty, noble perverts of the past would most certainly have admired.

I had, it seems, on my hands—or elsewhere, depending on the moment—a voluptuous athlete, vigorous in attitude, style, aptitude, and appetite. In his compact little frame he carried the freight of enthusiasm usually dealt out to many of larger, presumably more robust, constitutions. We were, in these antics, attracting considerable attention, not all of it as I mentioned earlier and judging by the proliferating scowls, favorable. But, in quick, gay reflection, we had paid our money—at least I had—and what we were doing was in keeping with the evenings activities—just look around!—and therefore nothing to curtail just out of deference for those with inclinations toward a more dignified propriety. I—we—might not be asked back but that was worry for another day.

"Hey, champ!" he cried.

"Yeah?" I replied.

"What say we go for the gold?"

"Yeah!"

And that's where the surprise came in.

In the most carefully calculated way, in the simplest of terms, in the grandest of schemes, it turned out that I'd been duped. I wasn't the cock of the walk, the bird of fancy feather, the soaring eagle free, all of these of my colorful perception. No. I was the pigeon, the goose, the chicken, and due now for the plucking, and with my newly found friend being the head plucker. It all happened so fast, so—God, I have to say it—captivatingly fast that even now I cannot remember exactly what happened. Or how. I can only say that in about the next eighteen minutes or so I had more dicks stuck into me in more holes in more combinations by more people than ever before during my considerable efforts along those lines. I was seized, teased, kissed, licked, sucked, fucked, rimmed, and browned. I was tickled, pinched, stretched, fingered, goosed, paddled, nipped, tripped, cuddled, primped, and spanked. And someone even cut a lock from my hair. Somebody liked my toes, and sucked them. Somebody liked my face, and sat on it. Another liked the feel of my hand, and dumped a load in it. I had cum on my chin, between my tits, on my dick, dripping from my balls and, needlessly said, my butthole was awash in the stuff. Assholes took my dick, my asshole took others, and once two at a time—or almost, but, sadly, too much. And then when I was sure that the only thing left to happen was a repeat performance, my impious little friend put his pretty black face— fuller now from the crass exertion—next to mine and smiled.

"Oh dear, do you like it?" he crooned.

I was speechless. All I could consider was kissing him.

"No, honey," he said. "We gonna make you come now."

Oh my.

Being held down, in fucking near-delirium, he started working me over with his hands—a lick and a sip here and there now and then for appearances—in the most excruciatingly deliberate masturbation in a history of memory harking back to age eight. Being denied control in any of its comforts, ignored in all its needs, forgotten in its cultivated pleasure, pushed to the limit, jerked from the summit, dangled in the crevasse, I was, dammit, on the very edge of agony, and kept there for just about as long as it takes two bugs to fart the national anthem—of Nepal.

"Like it, honeychile?" my friend asked.

I nodded, champ that I was.

Oh God, have you ever had someone pull your balls down tight so's the skin, oh that delicate, delicate skin, on the head of your dick shines like a heavenly marble, and then without much thought your lovely tormentor goes at it—like he's reading the fucking phone book—with a lot of spit and not much style—very slowly—until you think you'll go absolutely mad? It's really pretty neat. The main requirement is a capacity for endurance— all the way around—because it does take time. But boy, when the cards are dealt right, the hand played, and the chips are down it's a shot for a long memory!

Oh damn!

Prepared in hell, dressed in Hades, the rolling wash sloshed about in my belly just long enough to find the right hole and then, gathering a momentum from all the eruptions of the past and a few from the future, it started the slow spin upward, grabbing at my guts along the way, until it brimmed the container and sent the juicy smack sailing in its talented way toward the ceiling. My soul, aching for the companion of peace, twisted to be free of the monster, and, once released from its sticky grip, fell back in rubbery repose and vowed never, ever again.

Try it sometime.

I'm sure you'll like it.

So they left me there on that big work table—the site for preparing fancy pillows for fancy butts—to dry out and chill out, a certain amount of embarrassment causing a curling in my toes. Drunk—giddy—with fatigue I rolled into a sitting position, my legs dangling toward the floor, my cock between them, a little pissed off for now, and gazed at the boy still suspended, and alone, in the scaffold.

"Okay, fella, come on."

It was Jim, Tommy, and a couple of the other ring-leaders. In my dazed condition I was no match for them as they dragged me like a sodden circus roustabout to my next genital connection. The boy, somewhat limp from his ongoing ordeal, didn't really perk up when he saw them in the approach with me. But he didn't sag any further either. Someone, Tommy I think, thoughtfully brought a chair which he put before the boy. Without a whole lot of ceremony they plopped me over it so that I wound up with my ass so very conveniently within reach of the boy's pubis, his root emerging therefrom in a growing stir of interest.

"Better grease the dude up," somebody said.

"Nah, he's sloppy enough."

Well!

"C'mon, kid, this'll be your farewell performance."

I didn't think it'd take all those guys to get another cock up my ass, and it didn't really—they just wanted to make a show of it. And they did do that. With several others standing around and looking on and making sly comments they directed the boy's dick, a nice firm size come from the salami department, into the desired orifice. I thought I was past it, but the penetration sent that bubbly little I-wonder-why-I-do-this pain rippling out though my body to my fingers and toes.

Someone put a hand between my legs.

"I'll be dipped in shit, this guy's getting another fucking hard-on!"

I knew it! I just fucking knew it! Oh boy.

"Okay, kid, take this hotshot fucker down."

With the combined efforts of all and some well-meaning instructions from the kibitzers—hey! somebody put something hard in his fucking mouth—the lumbering debauch gradually took form and everybody all around rose to the occasion. I heard the clink and rattle of chains as the boy was released from his bondage to visit on me, as I'd already heard it said, his farewell performance. After a short celebration in which he beat his fists on my back like a tom-tom, he put his hands on my hips and started the ram on its final run to bring the fling to its neat close. It's the one old thing that doesn't get old, this fucking stuff. Hanging over that chair feeling not lovely, I was nonetheless flooded with a certain happiness, that foolish, useless happiness you feel—if you'll permit me a gross and inappropriate analogy—after taking an easy and abundant dump.

Ahem.

"Let me at 'im, dammit! I got all this shit started."

Yessir, it was my nemesis, the handsome black emissary from nowhere, standing in front of me, legs spread in authority, with his good-looking black dick, fully erected, in his hand.

"Gonna say good-bye soon, chile," he said, "but we gotta do this first."

165

Coaxing wasn't necessary. I just opened my mouth and it, that beautiful black dick, was in. So there I was, impaled, my peter in hard erection, and with a mouthful of cock—not an unenviable state but not one of startling uniqueness either—being pushed once again toward the launch pad for the unreachable outer limits. I was, in the gods' truth, getting awful tired. As I was fucked, I sucked. Somebody tried sucking me but that was a pretty hard job and he—they, whoever the hell it was—didn't last too long at it. And so settling in for the duration, I put my hands on my black friend's trim little ass and, in a wheedling little way, started messing around with his butthole. The response was good. Then, in something I had nothing at all to do with, somebody, Jim more than likely, started a fuck on the boy while he fucked me. Well, the boy—more than likely stoked to a smoldering flash point—started going crazy dancing a fuck jig in me like he'd never been up a butt before. I did everything I could to help out—churning, bucking, swinging... everything—and sure enough, just like geese laying speckled eggs, or whatever, the boy sang out one hell of a song—mercifully short—and went up on his toes, his nails digging into my sensitive butt, and just after he pulling out sent forth onto my broad, patient back for all the world to see, or at least those standing nearby, a huge stream of good old American jizz. And then he really did, for-the-life-of-Christ-and-all-His-horny friends, start to bawling, and really hard. Good Jim had to help him as he limped and staggered away, an already ancient veteran who'd seen much too much carnage. My friend, that *other* fellow, seeing his duty, took the matter in hand and, in a fine, expert manipulation, saw to it that his member of the delegation spoke up loud and long. I caught a good part of that speech—well, most of it—on my tongue.

Oh Lord.

Well, there were small exchanges of words, some personal muttering, hushed cries as a few of the other guys finished up their sweaty chores, and then in the general milling about quieting order came out of the drifting chaos as people began collecting themselves, their clothes, their satisfactions and dissatisfactions, and began putting an end, ready or not, to the affair.

Never really liking the closing of anything, I dressed in the angular shadows behind the piles of the naked polyfoam and, at a timely moment, slipped out through the metal door and into the early morning chill. I walked away fast, intent on nothing more than the walking which I wanted very badly.

A few cars passed.

A couple slowed.

I didn't look, so they went on.

As I walked, I collected myself and thought.

Of course I have no way of knowing how those gay Romans, or the queer Greeks either for that matter, might've felt after leaving an orgy. But I don't suppose a Roman mister tripping along the Via Satisfatica at about four-thirty a.m. on a Sunday morning two thousand years ago felt much different than *this* American one did doing that same stiff traipse up Cotillion Boulevard at the same time. I was amused, confused, grittily proud, snottily angry, hurt, and sore. If asked to define and document all those emotions in their twisted alliances I would have to, of course, somehow squirm out of the assignment. But I knew what I knew, dammit, and I knew what I felt, and, what's more, I knew all of it to be true, every damned bit of it. In my righteous stride I vowed that I'd sure as hell show them, by God. They could take their fifty dollar fuck parties and shove 'em! Shove 'em! Yeah! Thirty paces later along the asphalt, I thought, no, I'll go. Hell yes, I'll go. Fucking-a! But for one thing, I'll show up late. For another, I'll dress spiffy. I'll be cool. I'll be aloof. And I might not even *fuck* anybody, and I most *certainly* won't be fucked on a big, wide table by the whole goddamned horny troop, 'take a number, please'. Nossir, not me, not again. Fuck *them*. And further: if I ever get a-hold of the little black shit again I'll fuck him until his eyes turn blue and then take him out for breakfast where we'll have a long talk, get to be friends. And *then,* as far as Tommy and Jim *and* the pretty little brother—*if* he *was* the brother—are concerned, well, goddammit, I'll...

And so forth.

By the time I got to my street I had plowed and harrowed the ground pretty thoroughly, reaching absolutely no really perceptive—let alone concrete—conclusions that would stand up—and increase my popularity—in any positive social circumstance. If anything, after that sort of soul-searching walk I've always relearned just how precarious one's position is on the societal rack of things. Vigorous, breast-beating confrontations are not the best way to go. Golly, we see that all the time in the diets of crow eaten by the fallen amidst the hootings of those right then spared.

After a much needed shower I considered the pork 'n' bean situation, rejected it, and settled for some coffee and a couple of Tootsie Rolls. Then I went to bed, not exactly hungry. A stalwart fellow like me could hold out for another twenty-four hours or so. No problem there.

So, that was that.

At Alice's Cozy Pantry the next day, after working in a few bear claws, I set into my duties with my usual enthusiasm, an eye on the clock and the ham and eggs I was counting on during my break. I was sweeping the floor and doing the tidying things the boss likes to see.

"Hello, Scotch."

I turned around to a table situated in a small alcove. Dan was sitting there behind the clutter of the recently departed.

He hadn't been there three minutes before.

"Dan!"

Jesus, the old bowling ball of embarrassment knocked my pins right out from under me. Goddammit, I could feel a blush coming up and there wasn't anything I could do about it.

"How are you, Scotch?"

"I'm fine... okay. I'm okay," I stammered. "I'll get that stuff out of your way."

I started gathering up the dishes.

"You look sort of done out, Scotch."

"No! I'm okay. Really!"

"Sure?"

"Yeah."

"Okay."

While cleaning the table I took a sneaky opportunity or two to scan him more closely. He looked even thinner, trimmer, fitter than I remembered. He looked healthy and handsome.

I stowed the bus tub on my cart and scrubbed away with my towel.

Dan watched me.

"You don't have to say, Scotch, but why'd you run out on me?"

"Oh God, Dan, I feel like such as shit about that."

"Yes, I suppose you do."

"No, really. I'm sorry."

"Oh well, forget it. For someone like you, I suppose, there was no reason *not* to run out."

"That isn't true. No, it isn't." I tossed my towel into the tub. "Look, I have a break in about an hour. You want to talk a little then?"

Dan stood. His clothes were casual, neat, appropriate. He smiled.

"Yes, dammit," he said, "I'll talk to you."

"Good."

He came back at ten. I, of course, had to skip the ham and eggs. We sat at a back table, out of the way, by the broom closet.

"How's the job?" he asked.

I looked around the dining room. It wasn't a place to be ashamed of. Not by a long shot.

"Mine's fine," I said. "How's yours?"

"Okay. Well, better than okay."

"Good."

"I'm at the main office over here now."

"Oh," I said, kind of weak. "Hey, how about some more coffee?"

"No thank you."

Dan looked at me like he did when I was taking my clothes off at the motel.

"Why *did* you leave like that, Scotch?" he said. "Did I say or do something wrong? I thought things were going okay."

"They were, Dan. It wasn't you."

"Okay, if that's what you say, I believe you."

He took out his wallet and removed a card and handed it to me.

I glanced down at it.

Dan Gallagher

GULF STAKE & MONUMENT

Geology and Surveying

"I'm sober now," Dan said. "I'm in AA, but I still have a ways to go yet. I know that. I don't want to carry on like some silly sob sister about being sober, but it is very important. In fact, it's the most important change in my life I've ever made. Ever."

I nodded.

He made a motion toward the card and said, "Call me if you want."

He stood and then sat back down.

"You see, Scotch," he said, "in the time I spent with you I could see that I didn't really have to be drunk to be with somebody. There's a lot of different shit here but mainly because of you, in the long and the short of it, I'll never take another drink for the rest of my life. It's as simple as that. Yes, it's as simple as that."

He stood.

Putting a hand on my shoulder he said, "Call me when you feel like it, Scotch."

I stood up.

After we'd shaken hands and he'd gone, I sat down at the table in a goddamned daze! Somebody had actually told this lanky link from Pea Ridge, Kentucky that he 'in the long and the short of it' made a difference, that he was important, that he mattered.

That he mattered!

Well, I'll be goddamned!

I felt strange and very good. I felt far more important than if ten foxy dudes in a row had told me what a hot body I had.

I felt the opening of some kind of new chapter in my life.

I put my order in and sat at the counter looking at Dan's card.

I had no hard thoughts. There wasn't nothing to think really. I was just aware, and *keenly* aware, of me, of my job, of the cold coffee in the cups down there in my bus tub.

I was aware of life.

Me!

Scotch Wheat from Pea Ridge, Kentucky.

"Hey, fella," the cook yelled, "here's your ham 'n' eggs. Looks like you need 'em, buddy."

And, Jesus, let me tell you, those eggs tasted better than anything I'd ever eaten in my whole life.

Wonderful!

Well, as much as I'm inclined to anyway, I sort of floated through the rest of the day there at Alice's Cozy Pantry. Everything I did seemed important. Everything I'd always accepted as okay—like the way the milk is always cold even coming out of the dispenser the way it does—seemed not only okay, but almost perfect. And the way the salad room is always cooler than the rest of the kitchen. But then come three o'clock and the end of my shift and I was dressed in my Levis again and on the street and not really wanting to go home, I was visited once more by that vague feeling of meaninglessness. The streets, even there in the better upper reaches of town where the restaurant was, looked cluttered and mean and hard with the impersonal push and grab of all the stuff that makes up city life—and, mind you, I'm a guy who's pretty nuts about being in the city—and I wondered as I meandered toward *down* downtown if maybe I should set my sights a little higher in establishing my goals, which, I have to say, were next to being sort of nonexistent at the time.

What I mean is, was there any reason why I should be content in being a busboy and accepting all the stuff that goes along with being a busboy, like odd ball hours, surly waitresses, and snotty customers, and which is to say nothing about the low pay. Hell, just *considering* that low pay was the starting place on a whole ladder of dissatisfactions that I hadn't even started to climb yet. What I mean especially is that here was this guy—Dan—who was certainly a cut above most—oh hell, all!—of the guys I associated with, and who seemed more than a little bit interested in me. And so then why shouldn't I just kind of pursue the matter. Oh, not in any really expectant way of course, like heading toward *matrimony* or anything like that, but in the way of friendship and the like. You know, like having a guy to call on the phone and chat with now and then, and maybe make a date for seeing a movie every once in a while.

Nothing serious.

But then thinking again, not much of anything serious starts out being serious, does it?

I pulled Dan's card from my shirt pocket. It had looked impressive earlier, and now it looked even more so caught as I was in the throes of doubt in considering my own lack of stature.

My woeful—woeful!—lack of stature.

I saw a phone booth a ways down the street and I thought, well, kiddo, right now is as good as it's ever going to get.

So I walked right up, dropped a couple of coins in the slot, and punched the buttons.

"I'd like to speak to Dan Gallagher, please," I said.

In half a minute or so the dull flatness of nothing was broken with,

171

"This is Dan Gallagher."

"Dan, this is Scotch Wheat."

A pause.

"Why, Scotch! Golly, I'm glad you called."

"Am I interrupting anything?"

"No. I was just getting ready to leave. I have a meeting."

"Well, maybe I'd better call later."

"No! No! Look, maybe we could meet for a little while before I have to be there. The meeting I mean."

"Sure, that's okay."

"Great! How about on the corner like before?"

"That's okay."

"In fifteen minutes?"

"Okay."

"See you then."

"Okay."

Well, I really had to hustle my butt to get down to Eighth and Tucker in fifteen minutes, but I made it, and there, parked in a yellow zone, was Dan's red car.

Coming up from behind, I got right in.

After we'd exchanged hello's—not too stiff—Dan said, "I don't want to sound puffed up with importance or anything, but that meeting I mentioned is set for six." He looked at his watch. "And it's five oh five now, and it's a fifteen minute drive to get there."

"Not much time," I said.

"And, God, I'm getting a hard-on just sitting here next to you."

I put my hand between his legs.

"You're not *getting* a hard-on," I said. "You've got one."

Stick stiff in his slacks and pressed into his groin, that boner felt good under my hand. I squeezed.

"Oh it's *nice* and hard," I said.

"Oh golly, Scotch," Dan breathed softly, "I'd sure like to get that guy into some part of you."

I moved my hand to his knee.

"You could drive maybe three blocks down the street and turn right," I said. "Go under the overpass and up the ramp. There's a garage for a convalescent hospital there. Better skip the first level, but the second is almost always deserted."

"Got it."

Moving quietly into the street, the car carried us the three blocks to the turn. Making it, we surged down under some concrete abutments and then up the curving drive to the garage. After making two circles and a hard turn we came to a stop behind a dumpster and facing a blank gray wall with a chain link fence running in front of it.

Dan cut the ignition.

"Well now," he said smiling crookedly as if he'd been asked in to witness an execution.

Moving close and working fast, I opened his belt and fly and toiled and tugged trying to get his slacks and boxers down a ways.

The going was tough.

"Raise up," I said.

Dan raised his hips.

Still without a whole lot of room to work in, I did manage to get his pants and shorts almost to his knees. When he sank back, his bare butt squeaking on the rich leather, his cock, stiff and thick and ready, lay against the wheel. In the dim light cast of a hard and lonely space and the time running with fugitive necessity, it gleamed with invitation; it strained with immediacy. I took it in hand and pumped it slowly. Dan's hips pushed up joining in the ancient movement, and in those suggestive moves all the old tarnished magic found in sucking and fucking, and all the rest, was ready to be spun out again.

In fact there was more magic than we had time for.

"What I think I'd better do, Dan," I said, "is suck you off."

"Oh, be a baby and do that. Oh God, be my baby and suck me off."

I lowered my head and pressed my face to his belly, into his pubic hair. He smelled of wonderful, manly privacy, of the intimacy of dark closeness, of soap and sweat, and of the passage of silent, secret farts.

I kissed his cock along the shaft.

"Oh God, Scotch."

I ran my tongue up to the tuck beneath the head and pushed at the slit.

"Oh Scotch, baby."

His balls, now in a heated sag, lay in my palm. With two fingers pushing into the warm corridor, I rose up and went down, down on his cock and up, and down again. My lips a tight grommet about the shaft, my tongue a slick curl around the head, my throat was a berth for the stiff meat pushing up against me and into me. Oh man, I worked at the sucking of cock in the mission of squeeze, the squeezing pushing ever forward toward the wrench, the toss, the clatter, pushing forward toward the eruption of the hot jizzy discharge.

"That's the baby. Oh that's the baby."

Moving up the shaft, I pressed my lips into a tight seal around the collar and set my tongue against the hard knob in a stress of rough caresses with those followed by quick, stiff, licking strokes.

"Oh God, baby, that's good."

I sucked, twisting my mouth on the hot flesh, the blood stiff flesh.

"Suck me, baby. Suck me. Suck me. Suck me."

I slurped, curling my tongue around the head.

"That's the baby. Shit! Oh yes, that's the baby."

And I smooched, putting the kisses here and there, in his pubic hair, on his balls.

"Oh yes, kiss and suck, kiss and suck. Oh yes, baby."

Then I went down deep, the thick, witless tube filling my throat.

"Jesus, that's it! That's it, baby!"

I waited, stuck in the sweet terror between yawn and retch.

"Oh baby, it's coming."

I waited a little longer.

"Oh baby, it's here."

And, by God, it was too, and just gobs of it.

Pumped out in healthy surges—Dan moaning, his body stiff and jerking in the effort—the stuff was pushed into my throat by the throbbing lust of ejaculation. Using good control and maintaining my determination to deliver the very best possible thrill, I thwarted the retch by letting the jizz slide—oh man, thick, hot curds of it—down my gullet in one small slick swallow at a time.

And then, lying low in his lap and my tongue still pushing and pressing around in its sticky work, I waited until Dan's dick had gone soft and then raised up.

Dan smiled in that uncertain way and put his hand on my crotch.

"You're really hard," he said.

"That's what happens when I do this sort of thing."

Dan glanced at his watch.

"Oh shit," he said, grinning guiltily. "God, Scotch... Jesus, the damned time. I... I... "

"Oh hell, Dan, don't get hung up on things being handed out equal, like tit for tat. We did what we wanted to do, and I'm satisfied. Are you?"

"Oh hell yes."

And so Dan got busy putting himself together.

In a few minutes the car was purring in its quiet luxury and we went away from the low gray hulk of the parking garage. A few minutes more put us back on the street, back to where we started.

I opened the door, ready to make a clean getaway if need be.

"Wait a minute, Scotch."

I settled back a little thinking that maybe this was going to be the money part. The pay off. The kiss off.

"I want you to call me tomorrow morning," Dan said. "And dammit, Scotch, I mean it. You will, won't you?"

I nodded.

"Say you will, and say you promise you will."

"I promise I'll call."

"When?"

"Tomorrow morning."

"Okay, that's good." Dan put a hand on my knee and sent a hesitant smile. "I want things to be better than this. Better than in the car parked in a damned garage."

"Things don't always work the way we might want them."

"I guess that's right. But call me, okay?"

"Okay."

"Remember, Scotch, you promised."

I got out and stood on the curb as the car moved into traffic and away, that car a shiny red symbol of all the things I didn't have and probably wouldn't. But hell, I'd stood on the curb before, maybe not that very one, but on enough others, and more often than not after doing a little sucking or fucking, or both, and with, maybe, a steak in my belly and a twenty dollar bill or two in my pocket.

Oh yes, I knew where I stood all right. I took a certain pride in that.

But then again, I thought, this could be different. Anyhow it *seemed* like it could different. Dan didn't act like the usual sort of older guy on the prowl. I mean like being secretive and cynical. And he certainly hadn't offered me any money, or even hinted that he might.

I turned and started down the street. After a little ways I started thinking about maybe stopping by Hominy Bob's or Laredo. My nuts, don't you know, were still loaded up for a shot at the love target.

But something caused a little tinkle of a sort of quiet-like guilt to sound in my head.

I'd just been with Dan of course and, by and large, it'd been exciting enough considering the tough situation—in a *sports* car for Christ's sake—and yes I *did* have some sort of a date—a telephone date—for the next day. That was true. And then, on further thought, I was actually glad Dan hadn't offered me any money. That fact right there made his insistence that I call seem even more genuine.

So, all in all, it wasn't a *bad* deal.

And so, abiding by the clever convention of guilt, I made a fairly wide detour around the vicinity of the venues of fleshy pleasures known to me and went on home.

If I was making a fool of myself and even if in my own mind, there was an audience of only one.

Me.

The next morning during my break I called Dan. He really did sound glad that I called. Well, more than glad actually. He sounded almost, well, almost intimate, but in that cautious way that paves uncertainty with a degree of safety.

We exchanged a little small talk, familiar talk in short sentences.

And then...

"Say, Scotch," Dan said, "something kind of interesting came up at the meeting last night, something I think might be of interest to you."

"To me?"

"I think so. I'd like to tell you about it. Can you meet me tonight? And, believe me, I won't have to run off to another meeting. Maybe we can get something to eat. How about it?"

And so we set up another rendezvous.

We met at the usual—well, it was usual, sort of—place and after a short discussion about food preferences we decided on steak. That settled, Dan said he knew of a place called The Rustler's Rainbow which he thought I might like.

I said okay.

Well, The Rustler's Rainbow was a pretty nifty establishment, real classy and all done up in the western decor of leather and cactus and so forth, but all shiny and slick and bright with neon lights. It had that sort of edgy upfront look that's so popular these days.

Being that it was early we got a table right away. The cocktail waiter took our order for cokes and we started looking over the menu.

After a while Dan said. "I think I'll go for the lobster and filet deal."

"That sounds good to me too."

We sipped our cokes and in a little bit our food waiter came up, and I'll be a son of a bitch if it wasn't that good-looking black fellow of the Saturday night gang bang.

You remember him, don't you?

Well, sure enough he remembered me.

He gave me a smirky little smile, not obnoxious or anything like that, but familiar enough to establish a sort of communication beyond the matter at hand, that of food and drink. Dan might have caught it, but I don't think so because his smile was a lot more open.

"Good evening, rustlers," our waiter said. "My name's Clinton, and it's my pleasure to welcome you to The Rustler's Rainbow. I see you have your menus so I'll just give you a run down on our fresh veggies for tonight which are steamed zucchini with mushrooms, braised carrots with fresh pineapple, and creamed okra with water chestnuts. We have mashed potato, or baked. Or rice pilaf Stoloff, which is very good."

Clinton paused, and then said, "Are you ready to order, rustlers? Or shall I give you more time?"

"We're ready," Dan said.

We both ordered the lobster/filet combo, Dan going for the carrots, me for the zucchini. We both opted for the baked potato.

"Good enough," Clinton said. "Our sixty-four item salad bar awaits right over there and I'll bring you some cute little tubs of butter and a *huge* basket of bread. Do enjoy, happy rustlers."

177

Dan and I headed for the salad bar.

I don't understand the reasoning, if there is any, behind a salad bar. But that doesn't mean I don't like them. Actually I really go for the idea. It's just that... well, for instance, tomatoes don't really go with raisins, but there're both there. And how about chopped eggs and pineapple? Or chunks of jello and chili peppers? And so forth. What are you supposed to do when confronted with those conflicting choices? There should be a serene harmony in a salad, if you follow my meaning, and not a stylish sort of chaos.

Well anyhow, to avoid making a salad bar fool of myself in Dan's eyes I stuck to the stuff you'd most likely find in a tired, but tried and definitely true, salad at The Chat and Chew Cafe in Pea Ridge where they wouldn't have the slightest idea of what a salad bar might be.

When we got back to our table, Dan's salad didn't look a whole lot different than mine except he had a some applesauce plopped down right next to a stack of bean sprouts.

Our butter and bread—and it *was* a pretty big basket—had arrived as promised and so we began to eat.

I was curious about what Dan wanted to tell me regarding his meeting but since I didn't want to sound too inquisitive I kept quiet.

We munched and crunched along for a little while and then Dan cleared his throat.

"The company I work for," he said, "—well, actually it's my dad's—is doing a survey and stake out for a resort in the Keys."

"The Keys?"

"The Florida Keys."

"Oh."

"And I'll be going down there to work."

"I see."

"Oh, not permanently. At least not yet. This time it'll be just for a couple of weeks or so."

"I see."

Dan lay his fork down and pushed his plate aside.

"Scotch," he said, "I would like you to come with me."

The cherry tomato I'd just popped into my mouth suddenly seemed about the size of a watermelon.

178

"Me?" I mumbled.

Dan nodded.

I decided it best to do some chewing, and pretty quick swallowed the tomato, but with a little difficulty.

And then more composed I said, "Did I hear you say that you want me to go to Florida with you?"

"Yes. To Key West."

"For two weeks?"

"Yes, if you can swing it."

Jesus, I was dizzy with surprise. More than that, I was stunned. I mean, nobody'd ever asked me to go anywhere—not really—other than to the obvious places, like to bed and the such, and here—and pretty much out of the blue—I was being asked to go to a place of glamour and sophistication and distinction and, goddammit, remoteness!

"Oh my, Dan," I said. "I don't know what... "

Clinton arrived with out lobster and steak dinners.

"One for you," he said, "and one for you."

Decorated to please a queen, the plates gleamed with the gratification offered in an excess of plenty.

"What else can I bring you?" Clinton asked.

"Nothing right now, Clinton," Dan said. "Thanks."

"Then, rustlers, do enjoy."

I gazed on the plate before me shimmering with luxury.

"Is it okay?" Dan asked.

"Oh yes. It's perfect."

"Then let's dig in."

We did, and while I dug I thought about Florida, and all of what I didn't know about it. I mean like what would I *do* there? What would I say to the people there? What would I buy there? In other words, why would I go to Florida at all. And most of all, why would this handsome man, some years older than me, want to take me there?

After a while Dan said, "So what're your thoughts on the Florida idea, Scotch?"

"That's what I've been thinking about."

"I thought so. Well?"

"I want to go and I'd love to—Jesus, I'm surprised as hell—but I don't

179

know if I can. For the first thing, I have to think about is my job at Alice's. I just started there, you know, and I haven't got even one day coming as far as vacation time is concerned."

Dan nodded.

"Well, Scotch," he said, "I certainly don't want to diminish the importance of your job, but there could be another for you in Florida. And not in a restaurant either. I'm talking about a job on the project."

"A job on the building project?"

"That's right."

"Are you sure about that?"

"Reasonably sure. You see, I'm the fellow doing the hiring."

"Like you're the boss?"

"That's right," Dan said. "Okay, now here's the deal. I'm flying down Friday afternoon. Come down with me. I'll show you around and you can check things out. We'll swim some and enjoy the sun—and eat—while you get the feel of the place. But I want to point out that this is no glamour job we're talking about. It's hard work. For me and everybody else."

"Hard work, huh? What kind of hard work?"

"Site surveying. Basically it involves verifying monuments and boundaries and doing the staking. It's hard work but then it... "

"Count me in," I blurted, feeling immediately foolish.

"You didn't give me a chance to say that it pays well."

"Well, I'm still in," I repeated, now committed to my foolishness.

Dan laughed. "Okay. But come Monday and you don't think it's for you, I'll put you on the plane back here with no hard feelings and we're still friends. How about that?"

"It's a deal."

"And it's a good deal, I assure you."

While we finished eating, Dan filled me in on some of the more immediate details.

We'd leave Executive Airport at nine a.m. aboard, now get this, the company plane, and arrive in Key West around two in the afternoon. We'd be staying at the house of one of the developers—the major one—who'd been a friend of Dan's since college days. The house was on the beach and not far from the construction site so we'd have Friday afternoon and all day Saturday and Sunday to explore things while I got educated a little about the project and still have plenty of time for swimming and snorkeling, and maybe do some fishing. After all that, we'd talk things over Sunday night.

Oh man, it was a deal made in heaven, at least as viewed from the perspective offered there at that table in The Rustler's Rainbow. It wasn't that I was skeptical of Dan, or of his offer. I was just unsure of the goodwill of good fortune. I mean I'd been inflated with expectation before—but not for anything like this—and then unceremoniously dumped.

But then again, not enough to encourage suspicion for all time.

Fiddling with the few remaining decorations on my plate—I'd eaten everything that looked like it could be digested—I said, "It's a deal, Dan."

Like he was going to change his mind?

"You bet, Scotch," Dan said.

Pretty soon Clinton came by the table.

"Oh my, now weren't you a hungry rustler," he said, looking at me. "Your plate is practically *licked* clean."

"The food was very good," Dan said.

"It was," I agreed.

"Good," Clinton said. "Our desserts are simply fabulous too. Let's see, there's a hot apple pandowdy to die for, a chocolate custard cream Orleans rich enough to croak a cow, pecan pie straight from heaven, a six layer lemon chiffon cake fit for Marie Antoinette... "

"Please say no more," Dan implored. "I think I'll die for the apple pandowdy."

"And put me down for that lemon chiffon cake," I said.

"Would that be with ice cream, rustlers?"

"Yes, Clinton," Dan laughed, "with ice cream."

"*And*, rustlers, what *flavor* ice cream would that be?"

"Vanilla," I said.

"Vanilla," Dan said.

"And if you want," Clinton said, "I can bring chopped nuts, candied cherries, and some nice marshmallow fluff."

"Oh no, Clinton," Dan said. "Oh no, but thanks."

"You're sure?"

"Yes."

"Okay. But, all in all, rustlers, I'd say good choices all around," Clinton commented and went away.

181

"Nice enough fellow," Dan observed, "but I wish he'd stop calling us rustlers."

"Me too."

And pretty soon the nice enough fellow was back with desserts high and mighty enough to pacify the cravings of the greediest sweets junky.

Dan groaned.

"Now don't be that way, sweetie," Clinton said. "This ain't gonna hurt you none. This handsome rustler we got right here can work it off you. Can't you, chile?"

I nodded, my ears suddenly hot with blush. But not from Clinton's comment.

No, not that.

I was embarrassed inside for the curious pleasure I felt in having Dan and me considered a pair, a couple, even if by a waiter who depended on this sort of glib familiarity to help in making himself a living.

But still...

"Eat up, rustlers," Clinton said, "it's a long, hard ride you all have ahead."

Grinning, Dan and I took up our spoons, and Clinton, seeing his work there done, departed.

Later, the dishes cleared, our check retired to the cashier, and the unfinished coffee growing cold in our cups, we prepared to leave The Rustler's Rainbow.

Dan excused himself for the rest room.

Clinton sailed around the table and sat at Dan's place.

"Is this dude," he said, "your regular fella, or just a date?"

"I can't say yes to either one."

"Yeah, I figured that," Clinton said. "I ain't supposed to sit like this so I gotta make it quick. Are you up for us getting together some time?"

Jesus, again that feeling of undefined guilt—and this time like a small, velvet bomb—was set off in me.

"Golly, Clinton, I'd sure like to but... "

"I know, right now is a tough time to talk. Here's my phone number. I gotta go. 'Bye, chile."

And Clinton sailed away as fast as he had come.

I glanced at the number scrawled on a bar napkin and felt a certain satisfaction—another potential notch on my gun you might say. And yet I felt uneasy in that satisfaction, a new feeling for me.

I stuffed the napkin in my pocket just as Dan came around a thicket of pink sagebrush.

Outside, while we waited for the car to be brought around, Dan said, "Shall I drop you at your place, Scotch?"

"I don't really have anything to do there."

There was a long awkward pause as if some decision—even a vague one—had to be made.

"Well," Dan said, "we could go by the office and take a look at a few things concerning the project."

"Sure, I'd like that."

Dan's office was up high in one of the tallest buildings downtown, like on about the thirtieth floor. We rode up in an outside elevator. The view was terrific. The sun was at its lowest slant before falling behind the mountains and the city lights were coming on. In the quiet hubbub they cast jewels of winking color against the burnished gold of fading light.

"God, how different things look from up high," I said feeling very much the country bumpkin I am.

"It looks like it could be perfect, doesn't it," Dan said.

"Yes it does."

The elevator door opened into a sort of lobby area, except there wasn't much furniture—just a few expensive-looking iron chairs and low tables. But there were many large plants—*huge* plants—mainly palm trees, in big clay pots placed around. The place had class.

"This is it," Dan said, stopping at a ornately carved door.

He opened it and we stepped into a hush of elegance. Leather and fabric and mellow wood gleamed with the look of understated richness.

"It's some place you work in," I said.

"This is reception. I work back there." Dan pointed his thumb over his shoulder. "In a hole."

"I'd sure like to get a look at this hole."

"Okay. This way please."

Down a hallway and left past a cute little kitchen, Dan opened the door to a room stacked with books and binders, magazines and papers, and art and drawing paraphernalia all amid the clutter of industrious effort. The walls were hung with maps, photographs, and technical drawings.

"This is it," he said.

I took a turn around.

"I can't say that I understand much of what I see," I said, "but it's impressive as hell to look at."

"Over here," Dan said taking a few steps to a large flat table, "is the master plan for the Key West project."

I went to look.

And Dan pointed.

"That's the hotel there, and that's the public buildings housing the shops, theaters, restaurants, and the like," he said. "Then there's the cottages, the pool area, and the tennis courts." He moved a step. "And down here are more cottages and another pool, and then the beach area. Over there is the golf course."

"Golly," I said, "that's very nice."

"But of course there's nothing there yet."

"Nothing?"

"Nothing at all. Well, nothing but sandstone, the palmetto scrub, and of course the beach. We'll be about two months in the surveying and staking."

"And that's what I'd be involved in?"

"At first. You'd be the chainman."

"What's that?"

"That's the guy who lugs the rod and transit chain, and holds the pin."

"Is it complicated?"

"No."

"But it's pretty hard, you say?"

"Not really hard. Tough is more like it."

"Tough?"

"Yes. Tough."

"And I bet it's something you used to do," I said.

"I did."

Dan stepped behind me and put his hands on my shoulders.

"It's tough work that demands a tough fellow," he said. "A tough, able fellow with broad shoulders."

He ran his hands down my arms.

"And the arms on this tough fellow have to be strong."

His hands went to my waist.

"And the fellow has to be tall," he said, "and have slim hips."

His hands moved to my thighs.

"And," he said, "that's to say nothing about having strong legs."

His hands moved up and closed on my belt.

And I said, "How's about a horny fellow with a hard-on?"

"Not *you*?"

"Yes, me. And you too, I bet."

"I can't touch you without getting a hard-on."

I reached behind and felt, and it was hard all right. It felt good. Would it be, I thought, all right to do *it* here? right *here* is this serious, professional place? To find out—always clever in my instincts—I opened my pants and pushed them to my knees.

"Okay," I said, "what's your mood for a go at the cornhole?"

"Oh Jesus, I could happily die to get at that cornhole."

"No need for that, happily or otherwise."

"That's the boy."

After a moment's contest with his pants, Dan leaned into me, his hips pressed against my ass. His dick was pushed down between my buttocks, the head nudging at my nuts. He closed his arms across my chest and held me tight.

"Oh Christ, Scotch," he said into my ear, "I love holding you like this. I love holding you with my dick pushing at your butt and knowing that you'll let me, because you like me, get inside."

"Hell yes, you can get inside."

"Because you like me?"

"Well sure, because I like you, and because I like your dick too. But there isn't any choice to be made here."

Dan kissed my neck while making a few preliminary jabs at my asshole. His breath was soon coming in hot, quick pants.

"Oh Christ, Scotch," Dan said, "I could cream a load right now. Oh man. Oh Jesus."

"Oh Jesus is right," I said. "Let's get that charlie in there. Let's get that fucker in the cornhole."

"Oh yes, let's get that fucker in. Bend over for a cornholing, baby."

I bent down.

My face over the hotel drawing, my nose pointing at the pool, I reached behind and pulled open my buns feeling, as always, the sluttish luxury in offering up the rose once more for the fucking plucking.

"Get us some spit," I whispered.

"I'm getting it, baby," Dan mumbled.

Then I felt Dan's dick, the head a hard kernel designed for assault, pressed against the rose, and then pushed. There was the second or two of rubbery resistance, and then the wheels of lust, squealing with the jazzy thrill of anal pain, were on the round roll into the bliss of sodomy.

That tight brown rose was once again transformed into the cornhole.

My cornhole.

"Jesus Christ, it looks good," Dan said. "Oh God, I love to see your hard, round butt split open like that and taking my dick in the hole."

I pulled at my buttocks a little more.

"Oh yes," Dan said, "that's a beauty of an asshole stretched open, and hot and slick."

"And tight?"

"Oh yes, tight like a velvet noose."

"And ready to put out a good piece of ass?"

"The best piece of ass ever, baby."

Dan was running even in his strokes now, the moist push and suck of asshole and cock collecting, tingle by tingle and rub, the watery gremlins of ecstasy hidden within the impulses of love.

I worked rhythmic squeezes of my asshole—muscular little moves—on that wonderfully stiff cock, the slick tissues tightening and loosening their grip on the meat turning the screw.

"Oh baby, baby," Dan crooned.

I worked a few more.

"Oh baby," Dan crooned, "do it! Do it!"

And I worked a few more.

"Oh that's the ticket, baby. Oh yes! Oh yes! Oh yes, I got my prod up a sweet asshole. Oh yes, up a sweet asshole for the churning of some hot, creamy jizz."

And the prod, thick in the hole, pushed and pulled in the courting of the spew of that hot, creamy jizz. I felt, bent over with my butt split and my asshole at a slippery stretch, once again the endowment of glittering sin, the wealth of a whore born to this lewd freedom.

I worked again the magic of the anal squeezes.

"Oh fuck Jesus!" Dan cried. "Oh fuck Jesus, I'm coming. Jesus H. fucking Christ, take it! Take it!"

Humping into me, Dan pumped out the load, his body jerking in the triumph of release. Then, abrupt in his pull-out, he kicked out of his slacks and went to the floor. Rolling up on his back, he pulled his legs wide. His asshole, a prim pink pucker, lay there growing slippery in the jizzy drain from his cock.

"Take the hole," he hissed. "Take it and take it hard."

"It's going to be a trial," I said knowing that being cornholed isn't always that easy on a man who's just shot his wad.

"Forget that, baby. Take it!"

I gazed on this handsome man down before me, on the floor, his ass up, a piece of fuckable meat. There shone on his face a sort of sanctified greed. His blue eyes glittered.

"Fuck me good, Scotch," he whispered.

Going to my knees, I raised Dan's legs to my shoulders and put my cock, hard and dripping the silvery slime, against his anus and pushed. The entry a warm slick glide into the old smooth guilt of transgression, I went immediately to pelvic thrusts of steady rhythm. The pulse of the pumping was a perfect twist of lust and regard, for not only was my cock feasting on the meat found in the ditch of this man's asshole, I felt also the uncertain fluttering of affection seeking its own expression.

"Oh baby," Dan murmured, "this is the fucking I've always wanted. Fuck me and kiss me and kiss me and kiss me."

I moved easily into the kisses, Dan's lips soft and wet and warm and parted, his tongue slipping out and into a turning collision with mine. The muscle stiffened and I sucked it. It probed my lips and curled in my mouth, and I sucked it. Kissing lips and sucking tongue, I fucked asshole while our union—a wet formless surge—in this sweaty copulation was sealed with the spit of our kisses. Oh God, never before had I kissed with such lust and all the while that lust pushing gooses into love's pretty butt.

Dan moved his lips to my ear, nibbling and licking there.

"How'm I doing, baby?" he whispered.

187

"Good."

"Good? Only good? Well, how about this."

And then Dan turned the trick of the anal squeeze on me.

I was blasted with a tight jolt of indulgent dynamite.

"How was that, baby?" Dan whispered.

"Jesus!"

"Neat, huh?"

"Neat."

In my next thrust, Dan's asshole popped my dick fast with two, maybe three, squeezes.

"Okay, baby?"

"Okay!"

And then with flex after flex of the muscular hole Dan brought me to the thick, miasmic—though brief—passion of orgasm where the thrill of ejaculation was wed into an exquisite pain of passing folly.

I slumped into Dan's arms and where, spent and complete with the nuts and bolts of lust twisted to satisfaction, I soon found pleasant offers of more kisses, these now born of a gentle and playful nature.

Soon rousing ourselves, we rose and, in soft conversation, dressed.

I stood at a window looking onto the city, on the glittering throw of light across the sweep and eruption of its hard, relentless beauty and wondered where I actually stood in all this, in this endless riot of effort.

"Scotch."

I turned.

Now composed in capable authority, Dan was sitting at a desk.

"Scotch," he said, "I'm going to write out a check for you."

"A check for what?"

"Well... I guess for things you might need for the trip, or, well... "

"It's kind of isolated down there, isn't it? Where we'll be, I mean."

Dan laughed. "Well, yes it is."

"Then I don't need anything. I've got Levis and some tough work boots. I don't need much else, do I?"

"No."

"Then I don't need any money."

"Are you sure?"

"Very sure."

"Okay, if that's the way you want it," Dan said and stood up.

"That's the way I want it, Dan," I replied. "Believe me, I'm real excited about going down there to Key West with you and seeing about a job and all. But when I get money I want it to be money I've earned."

"I hear you, Scotch," Dan said. He came to me and put his hands on my shoulders.

"And I'll bet," he said, "you'll be going in to Alice's Cozy Pantry tomorrow, won't you?"

"Well, yes. I got to work my regular days. I'll tell them Thursday night that I might not be in Monday or Tuesday and see what they say. I don't want to just up and walk out on them, you know."

"I know."

Then Dan kissed me, lightly but very nicely, on the lips.

"Let's go," he said.

We came down out of the high rise luxury in the outside elevator, and again the city, in it's shimmer and the shine, glitter and glow, was startlingly impressive. In keeping with my growing sophistication, I tried not to stare.

For the first time I let Dan drive me home. He made no comments about the old three story houses—once the fancy of the uppercrust—with their beaten down yards and the bent and leaning chain link fences.

"It's that yellow one," I said.

Dan parked under a street lamp, the light bright on the red glamour of the car.

"Okay," he said. "I guess I won't see you until Friday morning."

"Right. Friday morning."

"It's about an hour or so out to the airport. I'll pick you up here at seven-thirty."

"Right."

"And you're sure you have everything you need?"

"Everything."

"Do you have swim trunks?"

"Yes."

A certain stiffness—the stiffness of expectation I guess—was creeping into our conversation.

"Well, then," Dan said, "I guess I'll see you Friday morning."

189

"Yes, Friday morning."

Feeling a new and warming sort of confidence I turned in the seat and put my arm across Dan's shoulders and kissed him.

Dan put his hand at the back of my head and pressed us deeper—and longer—into the kiss. It seemed a kiss born of the future.

Moving back, I opened the door. "Good night," I said. "And thank you. I'm looking forward to Friday."

"Good night, baby."

Standing on the curb, I closed the door. The car moved away and into warm dark night.

Turning, I went past the garbage cans, the blocked-up vehicles, the stack and tumble of discards—the broken clutter of urban apathy—and climbed the stairs, their deterioration a quiet creaking, to my little pad.

I sat for a while looking at the blank, glaring stare of my Salvation Army teevee.

Then I moved to my desk, fashioned of blocks and planks, and started to write.

It's close to six a.m. now. I've been writing all night getting this recorded. Pretty soon it'll be time to hike down to Alice's Cozy Pantry and get into the groove—nurture the enthusiasm don't you know—for hauling those dirty dishes, polishing the silver, and sweeping the floor.

Of course there isn't anything wrong with doing that for a living. Oh no. Back in Pea Ridge it'd be much better than all right. Oh yes.

But still, things could be better. Lots better. I don't spend a lot of time thinking about how to make things better, but I guess I should.

Well, come sometime Friday afternoon I'll be in Key West, Florida.

Me! Scotch Wheat!

And I'll be there with Dan Gallagher, a man of education and position, and with more than a little bit of money from the look of things. And who, more important that all that, seems to like what he sees in me.

Okay, that's good enough for now. Let's see what happens.

Still, it might be a new beginning.

Yes, we'll see what happens.

ADDITIONAL SEXY READING
BY
DIXON STALWARD

"PIECES"

Stalwards's first published book, and a classic. In eight short stories varying in length from twelve to sixty-two pages you will meet many more hot men as only Dixon Stalward can create them. A spicy diet of raunchy reading on 186 simmering pages.

"LEAPS"

Collected here are eight short stories of a most sophisticated persuasion. No library of gay erotica Americana is complete without this volume of ribald, fast, earthy, often wry, and very, very sexy tales. Steamy diversion of the very highest caliber. 196 pages.

"HORSES"

An episodic novel in five marvelous parts, the pages here are packed with rambunctious, bawdy men putting the moves together in dynamite action. Optimistic, positive, and wonderful, this is the gayest of all gay explicit fiction. 192 pages.

PLEASE USE ORDER FORM ON REVERSE

ORDER FORM

Name: _____

Street: _____

City: _____

State: _____ Zip: _____

□√ "PIECES"   □√ "LEAPS"   □√ "HORSES"

Each copy of each book is $12.95 plus $3.50 per book shipping and handling: (Shipping for overseas orders is $5.00 per book.)

$_____Number of books X $12.95

$_____Shipping, (Number of books X $3.50.)

$_____Add 7.75% sales tax to orders shipped to California addresses.

$_____Total amount enclosed

Please make check or money order payable to CABOOSE PRESS.

□ √MasterCard   □√ VISA   □√ American Express

Card Number:_____Exp.Date:_____

Name as it appears on card: _____

Please mail completed order form to:

CABOOSE PRESS

P.O. Box 567

Rocklin, CA 95677-0567

I certify that I am twenty-one years of age or older and that I am ordering this material for my own personal and private use.

_____

Signature